Praise for *Just Call Me Mike: A Journey to Actor and Activist*

"This is the most revealing and honest personal story that I have read in a long time. A genuine gem." —Senator George McGovern

"A simply told, extraordinary story. It is the best in storytelling, as if Farrell is sitting in the room with you." —*Los Angeles Free Press*

"These pages contain pure, luminous self-revelation . . . No one can read these pages and continue to live a narrow, anxious, self-absorbed life." —Sister Helen Prejean

"Farrell doesn't just take his case for human dignity and the value of life into the purified chambers of a liberal audience, but debates it in the unfriendly halls of those who are convinced that an eye for an eye is the way to go. He withstands shouts and vilification with an equanimity of spirit possessed only by those comfortable with their beliefs and willing to tolerate abuse on their behalf. It"s what makes a soul glow." —*Los Angeles Times*

"First of all, Mike Farrell is an honest guy. Then you add in that he's a stand-up guy as well. The combination means his book, *Just Call Me Mike,* will entertain and inform you far beyond most autobiographies. Farrell's life is fascinating and his journey is well worth your time." —Bill O'Reilly, anchor, FOX News Channel

"I've always just called him Mike. But now I have to call him talented, brave, principled, indefatigable, thoughtful, generous, and a man driven by his conscience. I learned things about him in this book I never knew before. So now I have to call him humble, too. He's really kind of irritating." —Alan Alda

"If you question why Hollywood actors get involved in politics, Mike Farrell can give you a whole book full of very persuasive answers . . . [An] engaging new memoir." —*Los Angeles CityBeat*

"In this honest autobiography, Farrell provides intimate accounts of growing up working class in the shadows of wealthy Hollywood, overcoming personal demons as he starts his acting career and finding happiness in the popular sitcom . . . His passionate descriptions of human rights abuses show why Farrell is considered one of Hollywood's most prominent activists." —*Publishers Weekly*

"After years of searching and some spectacular professional successes, Mike Farrell made an uncompromising commitment to his fiercest passion—a love of global fairness, collaboration, and civility. This is a fascinating account of that journey."

—Governor Mario Cuomo

"This informative, courageous, and sometimes scary account of the life of a modern American male grabs the attention early and never lets go."

—Sidney Poitier

"Take a break from the Paris-goes-to-jail countdown and read about a celebrity who's actually using his fame for good . . . He provides countless insights into our world and the nature of service. Five stars."

—*Hour* (Montreal)

"I admire Mike Farrell for his citizen activism. He has used the influence that accompanies his celebrity as a force for doing good, and the lasting impact of his humanitarian work is his legacy. The story of his rise to stardom and his commitment to service is inspiring."

—Rosalynn Carter

Just Call Me Mike is a riveting tale of personal, professional, and civic growth from sallow California kid to mature citizen committed to a more just social order. Whether Latin America, the Middle East, the death penalty, or a whole host of other human rights issues, Mike Farrell has confronted government abuse with courage, dedication, and tenacity. It is a life lived in a way that would make Voltaire proud. In short, I loved it."

—Ambassador Joseph C. Wilson, IV

"Mike Farrell's memoir is a sometimes funny but always serious development of a committed artist's life. Read it and enjoy—and wonder why there aren't more like him."

—Julian Bond, Chairman, NAACP

"Mike Farrell's personal journey is a wonder in itself. Those in the cultural community who have ever been concerned about the arts and political activism should have all their fears assuaged by this wonderful documentation."

—Harry Belafonte

"It's the illumination, the light that Mike Farrell kindles with his life, and the wonderful complexity of his humaneness that shine through this extraordinary book. It will ennoble and empower all who read it."

—Rabbi Leonard I. Beerman

"An inspirational tale of change for a wide audience, from prior fans of his career to new-comers ..."
—*Midwest Book Review*

"Mike Farrell's passion to discover, portray, and improve the human condition shines through his book and brings credit to his profession as an artist and as an activist."
—Warren Beatty

"Mike Farrell may be best known for his years on *M*A*S*H* and *Providence,* but his new book is no mere collection of show business anecdotes. It is the story of the merging of the personal and the political realms in one man's journey through life."
—*Mail Tribune* (Southern Oregon)

"I have long since come to understand and appreciate Mike Farrell's sincere devotion and commitment to justice, fairness, and equality. Despite being an accomplished actor and gaining notoriety as a human rights activist, he remains humble and focused. *Just Call Me Mike* confirms Mike's love and compassion for people. This book must be read by all of those who profess to be committed to First Amendment rights and human rights, but do not have the courage of their convictions to stand up and speak truth to power. Mike's work and courage puts us all to shame. We can all do better. Thank you, Mike."
—Congresswoman Maxine Waters

"Farrell doesn't hesitate to put himself on the line, whether writing about his troubled past, the behind-the-scenes conflicts on the *M*A*S*H* set, or his human rights activism."
—*Sacramento Bee*

"An intimate, compelling memoir by a popular actor and dedicated humanitarian, *Just Call Me Mike* is even more: It's an exciting page-turner, a modern spiritual odyssey, and, as the reader discovers, an account of one man's courageous battle against injustice in all its nefarious forms. Mike Farrell makes the world a better place—and this book may change your life."
—Donald Spoto, author of *Enchantment: The Life of Audrey Hepburn*

"Mike is one of the most gifted, committed, and interesting people I know. His book is a fascinating perspective on his own remarkable life, as well as our shared history. Full of great stories, valuable insights, and powerful inspiration."
—Bonnie Raitt

"In *Just Call Me Mike,* the author tells of his campaigns across our country and around the world on behalf of the poor, the forgotten, and the oppressed. To this battle, our modern

Don Quixote brings a skeptical intelligence, a disciplined passion, and an informed contempt for those in authority ever ready to sacrifice human rights on the altar of imperial ambition. Without boast or brag, *Just Call Me Mike* testifies to the vital role played by citizens who ennoble our nation by their willingness to denounce abuses of power."

—Ambassador Robert E. White

"Mike Farrell proves that ferocious conviction is the organizing principle of an extraordinary life. In his memoir, *Just Call Me Mike*, he describes the fantastic, sometimes painful, and ultimately redeeming journey that his conscience has led him on. Like his life, the book dances seamlessly between his great passions—from fond memories on the *M*A*S*H* set, to nervous moments at military checkpoints on his way to help refugees in war-torn Central America, to scrubbing-in for real-life surgery on a prisoner of war in El Salvador. In a disarmingly honest and gentle voice, *Just Call Me Mike* collects an incredible diversity of experiences, so diverse that it's difficult to believe that one person could accomplish so much, in art and in service to others."

—Kamala Harris, District Attorney of San Francisco

"With raw honesty as his constant companion, Mike Farrell reveals a journeyman's stirring quest for truth, which brought him to work tirelessly on human rights, protection of the environment, abolition of the death penalty, and so many other issues on behalf of the voiceless. *Just Call Me Mike* is a riveting read, and left me inspired by the determination of one person to create a more just world."

—Kerry Kennedy

"Incapable of putting his conscience on hold, Mike Farrell beautifully articulates why he is a rebel without a pause."

—Larry Gelbart

"Mike Farrell's passion for life and compassion for people are formidable. *Just Call Me Mike* is not merely an autobiography, but rather a road map and a book of directions for those desirous of affecting positive change. He makes believable the principle that one person CAN make a difference—we should all be that kind of citizen."

—Stanley K. Sheinbaum, economist

"Thoughtful and honest."

—*St. Paul Pioneer Press*

OF MULE
AND MAN

OF MULE AND MAN

MIKE FARRELL

Akashic Books
New York

Published by Akashic Books
©2009 Mike Farrell

ISBN-13: 978-1-933354-75-0
Library of Congress Control Number: 2008937350

First printing

Akashic Books
PO Box 1456
New York, NY 10009
info@akashicbooks.com
www.akashicbooks.com

To Shelley,
from the luckiest man in the world

And to Mule,
for bringing me home to her

ACKNOWLEDGMENTS

Absent two things, you wouldn't be reading this. I am deeply grateful for both.

One is the dedication, faith, trust and genius of Johnny, Johanna, Aaron, and Ibrahim at Akashic Books. This fearless, audacious quartet makes the impossible possible.

The other is the sweet, irascible, shy, pushy, obedient, demanding, uncomplaining, touchy, indefatigable, fierce, valiant entity that stormed into my heart as it kept me safe, sane, warm, dry and protected against whatever the gods chose to throw our way. Contrary to its every instinct—traits many will claim it does not possess—it did this not only because it was the task assigned, but because, in a manner it will deny and many will have difficulty accepting, it loved me. But for Mule, this book would not exist.

TABLE OF CONTENTS

On Saturday, May 10, 2008, Mike Farrell set out on an 8,882-mile, twenty-five-city book tour to promote the publication of the paperback edition of his memoir, Just Call Me Mike: A Journey to Actor and Activist. *As the American presidential race kicked into high gear, Mike drove himself across the country and back, networking with the human rights and social justice organizations sponsoring each event along the way. Following are his tour dispatches.*

INTRODUCTION

April 2009

Los Angeles, CA

Do you know about serendipity? Well, you're holding it in your hands. The word has always tickled me—as does the sense of wonder that comes from having amazing things happen or discoveries made, quite spontaneously, as if by accident. This book is all of that—all part of a kind of magical experience. I had no intention of writing my first book—the one from which this one has sprung (but that's another story)—so just imagine my delight at the birth of *Of Mule and Man*.

Writing *Just Call Me Mike: A Journey to Actor and Activist* was an adventure in itself, one for which I'm enormously grateful. But the process of introducing it to people, the "book tour" effort necessary to allow an offering from an independent publisher to get a modicum of attention in an extraordinarily competitive marketplace, has not only been a surprise, it has turned into one of the great treats of my life. With every stop on the tour cosponsored by individuals or groups I've worked with in efforts to secure social justice across the world, these travels have been a great way to say thanks to them, and thanks to America for giving us a reason to believe a just society is possible. And the openness and willingness of people across the U.S.—in so-called red and blue states—to welcome me, to come and say hello, to accept the invitation to hear what I have to say, has enriched me in ways not easily put into words.

That being the case, the chance to do a second tour, this time with the paperback release of *Just Call Me Mike*, was too good an opportunity to resist. And little did I know, when Johnny Temple, the publisher, asked me to write a journal of the experience for the *Huffington Post*, that this larky diary would turn into this chronicle, this multifaceted tale of an adventure, an odd kind of love story, and, in all, a heart-wrenching, mind-altering, spirit-raising, brain-twisting happening. It's a story of what was a total hoot!

From California to the New York Island, as Woody Guthrie sang it, my . . . well, I'll leave it to you to figure out what she/he was to me . . . Mule and I traveled the highways and byways of this great nation—and back again. We saw the high country and the low, the deserts and mountains, the rusty, dusty, boarded-up towns and the bright, shiny, skyscraper-laden cities. We saw extraordinary beauty, natural and otherwise, the horror wrought by Hurricane Katrina, the waste laid by the Iraq War, the remnants of the industrial strength that once powered our nation, the changes caused by global warming, the homeless who've been left out and the hopeful who believe it can yet be made right.

I found long-lost friends and made new ones, discovered long-lost relatives and reclaimed them. I saw evidence—everywhere—of the loving embrace *M*A*S*H* enjoys. So many people came out to laugh with me over memories of the television show, and also to share stories of first watching it with their mothers and fathers or grandparents and now doing the same with their children and grandchildren; it touched me deeply. The connection, it was never more clear, between countless numbers of people and that show, is engraved on their hearts—as it is on mine.

And in every place Mule and I stopped there were books and book people, readers and writers and those who love words. We talked show business and politics, social concerns and personal ones. Poets and students, the young and the old, were all joined in a mutual sense of gratitude for the possibility of human survival that is promised in the millions and millions of words around us, words written by cynics and lovers, the great and the small, the hopeful and the hopeless, all with a need to put down thoughts, to leave some trace of themselves, for the benefit of those who come after. (As with my first national book tour, political and social justice groups cosponsored each event. You will find details about some of them in the pages that follow—often in their own words—along with a Resource Guide at the end of the book with contact information for all of them.)

These bookstores and libraries are temples, in a way, even the glittering chain stores, to some degree, but mostly the struggling little independents, the mom-and-pop stores; these places, run by big-hearted, literature-loving souls who relish bathing in human knowledge, are havens for the world's seekers. Those who prowl the stacks gain confidence that there is a reason for being—for some, that there is finally a purpose to their existence—by delving into the hearts and minds, the thoughts, ideas and ideals of human beings courageous enough to set them down for others to touch, consider, take in, laugh at, accept, reject, enjoy, identify with and, as a result, become more than they were.

In that spirit I welcome you to this whimsical journey that I shared with a . . . well, with a machine . . . an inanimate object that became . . . animate. It became Mule: my friend, my companion, someone I loved.

This is a mostly lighthearted sharing of a fabulous trip. It was a wacky time, but if there are laughs, and I trust there are, there are also discoveries, some hopefully thoughtful observations and some wonderful experiences, all of them part of coming into contact with the decency, generosity and hope that are, to me, the spirit of America.

Mike Farrell
Los Angeles, CA

DAY ONE
Saturday, May 10, 2008

CITY OF ORIGIN: LOS ANGELES, CA

MILES TRAVELED: 382

CITY OF DESTINATION: TEMPE, AZ

VENUE: CHANGING HANDS BOOKSTORE

EVENT COSPONSORS
Veterans for Peace, Coalition of Arizonans to Abolish the Death Penalty

W ell, this isn't the way it was supposed to work.

This marathon tour, this 8,000-mile drive across the country and back to promote the paperback release of *Just Call Me Mike: A Journey to Actor and Activist,* was supposed to be a great adventure that my wife, actress Shelley Fabares, and I would share, a month-long odyssey of laughing and looking, seeing new places and old ones, meeting new people and old friends and just loving being together.

But it wasn't to be.

The timing had been perfect: we'd take off just a week after my son Michael married his sweetheart, Peggy, in our backyard. It would be tight, yes, working out all the craziness of a large wedding and the logistics of this trip (not to mention Shelley's inevitable all-night pre-trip packing frenzy), but nothing could stop us.

Not so fast, Johnson!

A few days before the wedding, while outside hosing off the side of the house to make it more presentable for the soon-to-be-gathering multitude, Shelley was startled by an unexpected squirt of water in the face, lost her balance and fell.

Paramedics, the ER, the X-ray, the news of a badly broken hip, admission to the hospital and hip-replacement surgery soon had my head spinning, reconsidering everything. The wedding must go forward, of course, but could Shelley be there? Unfortunately, as it turned out, she could not. (Though a sweetly generous gesture by Peggy, who swept into the hospital room in her wedding gown, and a cell phone placed in front of a speaker during the ceremony, made Shelley very much a part of it.)

And what of this long, well-organized, meticulously planned book tour, with dozens of appearances scheduled, commitments to stores carefully arranged, and a raft of cosponsoring political and social justice organizations signed on? Could it be canceled, delayed, adjusted?

Yes, of course, said the good people at Akashic Books with a gulp; they'd figure something out. Not a chance! said Shelley. She'd be fine. She'd be up and doing her physical therapy, she'd be supported by our family and our friends, and I had to get the hell out of town.

Well, it was certainly more complicated than that, but this is the gist of it. And here I am.

After picking up a rented Prius at LAX airport—the insane price of gas demanding a hybrid—and quickly throwing everything I could think of into a couple of bags, I took off this morning for the first stop: Changing Hands Bookstore in Tempe, Arizona, just outside of Phoenix.

Driving east on Interstate 10 quickly takes you into the incredibly frightening air of the San Gabriel Valley. I keep thinking the smog in the

San Fernando Valley is scary, but at least it gets blown away periodically. This stuff you can cut with a knife.

Past orchards of windmills and into the desert, the haze thins out and the landscape grabs you. I've never been one to appreciate the particular beauty of the desert, but today it impresses. It is so clearly harsh, so openly hostile to all but the most hardy adventurer, that it proclaims itself with an impressive hauteur that has, I must admit, a kind of arrogant beauty. Don't fuck with me, pal, it seems to be saying.

As I careen along, trying to figure out what means what on the odd dashboard in this strange car—this is my first experience with a hybrid—I keep watching the gas gauge, remembering that the last time I came this way I had to stop and fill up in Desert Center, a particularly hot and unforgiving place that one in need of fuel is strangely happy to discover (but doesn't want to use the facilities). Yet the gauge doesn't seem to have moved, making me wonder if I'm looking at the right thing. That does appear to be a little gas pump on it, I reassure myself, so what else could it be?

What else could it be, indeed? It could be any damned thing, I tell myself, recalling that when I first got in the car I couldn't figure out how to start it, much less make it go. Embarrassed, I had to go find an attendant to show me how to make the bloody thing work.

This Prius doesn't even have a key! Who knew you had to stick the square thing in the hole and push? And there's no gearshift! There's just a little kind of funky plastic knob on a stick—a short stick, at that—which kind of wiggles up and down. And a button you push for *Park*. I assume that means the gear, *Park*, which means you stand still, but I was already standing still. I wanted to go!

So, like I'm an idiot, the attendant shows me that you push in the square thing, then you have to push the button that says *Power*. (Now, of course, being able to read, I had already tried that, but nothing seemed to happen.) Ah, but you have to step on the brake when you do it! Uh-huh. Then, as he points out, the dashboard lights go on and with them a little red thing that says *Ready*!

Uh-huh. But when I step on the accelerator, nothing happens. That's because it's not in gear. Uh-huh. How do I get it in gear? You jiggle the funky plastic knob on the short stick. Up to go backward, down to go forward. Uh-huh. But nothing is happening. That's because you're not stepping on the brake. Huh? I have to step on the brake to shift? Right. Uh-huh.

So, despite the fact that I can't hear an engine running, I step on the brake, pull the funky little plastic knob on a short stick down, step on that gas and . . .

Here I am.

Bing! One of the little squares on what looks like it must be a gas gauge goes away, telling me that some gas is being used. This I can understand because it's like the one on my motorcycle. But, like the one on my motorcycle, I'm not sure how much gas each little square represents. Oh well, on I go.

COALITION OF ARIZONANS TO ABOLISH THE DEATH PENALTY

The Coalition of Arizonans to Abolish the Death Penalty is a group of organizations and individuals committed to ending the death penalty in Arizona. We are the oldest anti–death penalty group in Arizona and an affiliate of the National Coalition to Abolish the Death Penalty. Our activism has helped abolish the death penalty for the developmentally disabled—even before the U.S. Supreme Court prohibition—and for juveniles.

In 2008, Mike Farrell gave a keynote speech at "Writing Down Death," an event that featured authors opposed to the death penalty. Joining Mike were MacArthur Fellowship recipient Leslie Marmon Silko along with John M. Johnson and Rudolph J. Gerber, coauthors of *The Top Ten Death Penalty Myths*.

We welcome volunteers, members, and even just individuals who want to learn about Arizona's death penalty. Among us are those who oppose the death penalty for spiritual, ethical, and practical reasons,

And you know what? Less than six hours after leaving home I'm through Phoenix, turning into the motel in Tempe, and there are still two little squares on that line. All the way from Los Angeles to Phoenix on one tank of gas! I'm impressed.

and those who may choose variously to work for its abolition through prayer, self- and public education, dialogues, constitutional recourse, and public action.

We affirm the dignity and rights of victims and the right of communities to live in safety and harmony. We believe that the death penalty, by implicitly condoning killing, subverts these rights and contributes to a pervasive climate of violence.

The taking of human life is abhorrent and unacceptable to us; it assails each of us individually and diminishes us as a people. When the state takes a life, we are profoundly affected. We become participants in what we abhor. Moreover, we know that, being human, we are not above error. We would not commit irrevocable error. Our sense of shared humanity, our commitment to the creative and transforming spirit that links us, and our knowledge of our own fallibility call out for us to discover and use alternatives to capital punishment.

In pursuit of our common goal, we commit ourselves to nonviolence, civility of discourse, respect for those who hold opposite opinions, and faithful and persistent witness.

The event at Changing Hands is astonishing. Over a hundred people are there to say hello and hear me, including people from Code Pink, the Coalition of Arizonans to Abolish the Death Penalty (CAADP), and Veterans for Peace. As part of the introduction, I'm presented an award by Veterans for Peace: a beautiful statuette of a hand giving the peace sign. Though I'd been warned to expect something, this is a huge and very moving surprise.

The discussion, mostly Q&A, goes on for quite awhile and covers a broad range of subjects, from the war to the death penalty, prisons, *M*A*S*H*, Hollywood, politics, kids, values, my personal life and how we take back our country. The first question, though, was about Shelley, which gave me an opportunity to tell them why she wasn't here, as planned.

Nice people. A lovely evening.

Day Two
Sunday, May 11, 2008 (Mother's Day)

City of Origin: Tempe, AZ

Miles Traveled: 109

City of Destination: Tucson, AZ

Venue: Barnes & Noble—Eastside

Event Cosponsor
Coalition of Arizonans to Abolish the Death Penalty

Happy Mother's Day, sweetheart! The day begins with an old friend. Rick and I grew up together, and when I joined the Marines in 1957 as a buck private he had the audacity to get an appointment to West Point. We stayed in touch for a while but lost contact over thirty years ago, only to reconnect because he heard mention of my coming to town and sent a message to the manager of Changing Hands, the bookstore last night.

A couple of hours over orange juice provides time for a quick race through three decades, but I've got to make tracks for Tucson. Now living in a house he built in the wonderfully named Carefree, Arizona, he seems to be doing well. Rick still has that same offbeat sense of humor I remember as a kid. And now that he knows of the yearly reunions of the club that protected and sustained us through our school years, he'll try to make it to the next one.

Back on 10E out of Phoenix, I'm reminded that the sheriff of Maricopa

County is that cheap self-promotion machine, Joe Arpaio, the media hog who dubs himself "America's Toughest Sheriff." I spent a day at his prison a few years ago with the old Bill Maher show and found him to be every bit the "megalomaniac, liar and bully" *Harper's Magazine* labeled him. He's popular with the voters because he plays on their fears, and his bluster and bravado keep his name in the press and get him reelected. It's like Cheney and Bush playing the fear game with terrorism. Given to heaping abuse on those under his control, Arpaio plays into the idiotic notion that you can correct the behavior of inmates through humiliation and brutalization while diverting potential law-breakers with the threat of dehumanization. Scorned by human rights groups and those who champion decency, Arpaio is a blight on the very idea of "corrections" and an insult to intelligent law enforcement, just one step out of the cave and moving in the wrong direction.

Leaving the Superstition Mountains behind, I head down the long, flat highway through the Sonoran Desert toward the sharp, saw-toothed Santa Catalinas and, beyond them, Tucson. Along the way the occasional slopes to each side are dotted with a huge population of what to the casual observer might look like strange, tall beings waving hello. The saguaro cactus is said to appear nowhere else on earth but in this southwestern desert.

I figure the least one can do is wave back.

Suddenly this car, to which I'm only slowly becoming accustomed, begins a rhythmic beeping. Jarring enough, because a sudden outburst of beeping can't mean anything good as one is racing down the highway, it becomes even more frightening as the beeps speed up, getting closer and closer together. In the movies, this means a bomb is about to go off. Frantic, I look around and see no signs of distress or alarm on the dash or anywhere else; I check my cell phone, though I know that's not it; and I begin to slow and pull over as the beeps reach a crescendo and, just as suddenly as they began, stop.

Goddamnit! This car is messing with me! This is unnerving as hell. Then, panic subsiding, I move back into the lane and resume speed as I go over everything I can think of that might be responsible. Finally, on the far right side of the dash I see a red light indicating that the passenger seat belt isn't fastened. No one being in the seat, I hadn't thought to fasten it, even though I did set one of my bags there. It's a light bag, but could that be it? And why, if so, did it wait until now to yell at me? Did it let me know when I started out and I somehow missed it? Was it stewing about it all this time and then suddenly decided to give me hell? Man, this car is one temperamental sucker! I'm going to have to be careful.

Credit where due, I did discover something very interesting about the car—actually very cool. In the middle of the dash is a screen that, if you mess with the buttons around it, gives you all kinds of confusing information, complete with even more confusing diagrams. It'll tell you how much mileage you're getting at any given moment; it offers a very complex picture of the power train, apparently explaining the system by which the car is sometimes powered by battery and sometimes by the regular old-fashioned internal-combustion engine. These things are just obscure enough to drive a newcomer to the world of hybrids a bit mad, yet intriguing enough to pull your attention away from the road and get you killed. But that's not the cool part. The cool part is when you pull up the funky plastic knob on the short stick and put the car in reverse (after, of course, putting your foot on the brake), the screen in the center of the dash becomes a picture of what's behind you! So you can see where you're going as you back up. Though because the picture is a bit distorted, I still prefer to turn and look out the back window. But it is cool.

Coming into Tucson I make my way to the Barnes & Noble bookstore where I'm to do my thing—this one an afternoon gig. Since it's Mother's Day I doubt there will be a large crowd, but one never knows. Being a bit early, I check in and then go to a bar across the parking lot to watch most of the first half of the Lakers/Jazz fourth playoff game. Tied at the half by one of Kobe Bryant's impossible shots. (I later learn we lost in overtime.)

Back in the store, I am surprised to find a very nice crowd of over a hundred people, including some from the Coalition of Arizonans to Abolish the Death Penalty and a few others with whom I had worked in the Sanctuary movement in the 1980s. The movement, started by John Fife, minister of Tucson's Southside Presbyterian Church, a Quaker named Jim Corbett, and a few nuns, priests, other clergy and laypeople, believed that those coming across the border fleeing murder, torture, and mayhem in El Salvador and Guatemala deserved to be treated humanely and given shelter—as international law requires—rather than labeled as "Communists" and sent back to their deaths. The Sanctuary movement became a modern version of the Underground Railroad from the days of slavery, ultimately involving more than five hundred churches and synagogues nationwide. And for their trouble, these simple, decent people were arrested, tried, convicted and, probably because of embarrassment on the part of authorities forced to carry out the Reagan administration's paranoiac anticommunist zealotry, sentenced mostly to five years of probation.

Today, John Fife and many of these people are still at it, having formed the Samaritan Patrol, part of the No More Deaths movement. They go out and provide food, water, and sometimes directions to impoverished people attempting to make their way across the desert in search of work. The goal is to protect these poor folks from death by dehydration or starvation and occasionally to provide witness and help them avoid confrontation by Minutemen and others inspired by the racist raving of the Lou Dobbses, Bill O'Reillys, and Tom Tancredos intent on saving America from "mongrelization."

Again, we spend an hour and a half or so talking about my book, Hollywood, the death penalty, politics, this bloody awful war and a lot of *M*A*S*H*.

DAY THREE
Monday, May 12, 2008

CITY OF ORIGIN: TUCSON, AZ

MILES TRAVELED: 317

CITY OF DESTINATION: EL PASO, TX

VENUE: BARNES & NOBLE—SUNLAND PARK

EVENT COSPONSOR
El Pasoans Against the Death Penalty

Okay, a new day and we're to head for El Paso, Texas. But this hybrid and I are starting off with a new relationship. First, I have to say I'm very impressed that the little line of squares that tells me how much gas has been used hasn't moved at all. None of them have disappeared. None! I only filled up once, in Tempe, after arriving there Saturday night, and we've come over a hundred miles from Phoenix to get here (then more after the book gig yesterday afternoon when I got pretty well lost trying to find a much-touted restaurant up in the hills on Skyline Drive, but I finally figured it out). So, if I read this gas gauge thing correctly, it says we got here from Phoenix without using any fuel at all!

Whatever, I'm impressed with this rig; I admit it. So, I've been thinking over our relationship and I've decided I haven't been fair. I've been looking at the hybrid as a car . . . like, you know, a *car*. But it's a hybrid. Like a mule. And like a mule it can do a lot of work, maybe as much work as a pack horse, but it's not a horse, it's a mule. And a mule can be contrary and confusing and a pain in the ass, but if you don't expect it to be a horse you won't be surprised when it gets weird and obstinate. Right?

Right. So, off we go, the hybrid and I, on down 10E toward El Paso with, according to the little squares on the dash, a still-full tank of gas.

The land south of Tucson is very flat but doesn't seem to be peopled with as many saguaros as before. In fact, I don't see any. Maybe they're all at the convention up north. Before long the flat land gives way to a sort of rolling, undulating topography (don't you just love to use a word like that in a sentence?), and as I'm watching the speed, keeping an eye on the little squares (still all there) and noting the slight changes in the landscape, suddenly I hear three distinct beeps. With the first one I start to panic, with the second I look to see that the passenger seat belt is still fastened from the other day, and with the third I begin to decelerate . . . But . . . there's no fourth. Just three damned beeps! And then nothing. Nothing at all. There appears to be no problem. So I take a deep breath and think about it. The beeps seemed to be slightly lower in tone than the A-bomb alert from Saturday. There's no damned reason for them. It's just trying to get to me. It's a mule.

After undulating for a few miles, we come around a bend and begin a long descent into a deep, wide valley. It's kind of amazing to see, because everything has been so relatively flat for the last couple of days that I assumed we were at, like, sea level, but this grade will probably bottom out at 500 to 1,000 feet below where it started. And it's getting windy, pushing us around a bit. Mule doesn't like it.

Before long, we approach the Continental Divide. It seems funny to have the Continental Divide be so far west. We're only a bit more than 700 miles from the West Coast, so you'd think the CD would be closer to the middle of the country. But go figure. It probably has more to do with the Rocky Mountains and which ocean the waters drain into.

The air is very brown down here. I saw that in Phoenix too, making a snarky comment about smog, and my friend Rick said that a good part of it was dust from the desert floor kicked up by the wind. But, he added, smiling, it's also smog. Down here, as we settle into the floor of this valley, the dust is blowing pretty well and signs warn of dust storms and the possibility of zero visibility.

Pulling up into the hills on the other side of this broad valley, there's a phenomenal area that looks like a giant's playground; instead of regular hills made up of solid masses of dirt and impacted stone, these are great piles of rounded rocks that look like some huge kid played with them, rolled them around and stacked them. It's really quite spectacular.

Entering New Mexico, it's dry and flat and windy as hell, with giant dust devils hundreds of feet high off to the side of the road twirling like brownish-red mini-cyclones. I note the political tone down here, writ large on a huge billboard that says, *ONE NATION—UNDER GOD.*

After some miles I feel the need for a bathroom break. A couple of squares have disappeared by now, but there's no apparent need for gas, so I park by a truck stop. Inside, as I walk toward the restroom, three guys, two older and one younger, are behind the counter having a spirited conversation, with the young one saying, "It's comin', I'm just waitin' for it." The older of the three says, "These earthquakes and these storms . . ." I want to stop and listen, but can't, so go on into the men's room and wonder what they're talking about. When I come out, the young one is saying, "McCain's just gonna keep doin' the same thing." The older one seems to be in agreement and adds, "Yeah, I don't know if Obama can do everything he says he will, but I'm willing to roll the dice."

Grinning with surprise, I go out, fire up the mule, get back on the highway and turn on the radio. Only a few stations are coming in, but I find the dulcet tones of Rush Limbaugh and listen for as long as I can stand it. Clear Channel then provides The Choirboy, Sean Hannity, telling me they're "putting the Stop Hillary Express to bed and ratcheting up the Stop Obama Express." I consider calling him about the guys at the truck stop, but decide not to bother.

The wind blows us through Las Cruces and over the border into Texas and on to El Paso. Looking off to the south as you near the city, the incredible poverty of Juárez, Mexico is just a stone's throw away, right down below the highway and across the Rio Grande. It's dramatic, and heartbreaking.

Pulling into the downtown hotel I see that there are still four little

El Pasoans Against the Death Penalty

Michigan abolished capital punishment in 1847. When Carol Tures moved with her family from Michigan to El Paso, she was dismayed to find out that Texas carries out more executions each year than any other state in the U.S. In 2000, she called a series of meetings where people could hear speakers and discuss the issue. Before long, the audience became an organized group under the name El Pasoans Against the Death Penalty.

In the ensuing years, the group has sponsored several major events in cooperation with the Texas Coalition to Abolish the Death Penalty. One of these was "Journey of Hope," featuring talks by family members of murder victims and of persons who have been executed. Another was "Music for Life," part of a statewide tour in which Sara Hickman from Austin entertained audiences with her songs and moved them with her simple testimony. The group has also distributed literature to people reporting for jury duty and has remembered murder victims, offenders, executioners, and their families in monthly vigils in front of the county courthouse. Its most recent undertaking is "Birthday Cards for Death Row," based on a project begun by Betsey Wright of Arkansas. Carol Tures and her family left Texas recently, and now her work continues both in El Paso and in Nashville, Tennessee.

squares on the gas gauge. All the way from Phoenix with a stopover in Tucson and here we are in El Paso with gas to spare. This mule is skittish and contrary, but damn, it's practical.

The book event at Barnes & Noble here is a tonic. This whole celebrity thing continues to boggle my mind. Pulling into a strange city, knowing no one, and having a large group of strangers waiting, apparently happily, to see you is . . . well, it's hard to explain how it feels. Men and women, young and old, a mix of ethnicities, and they're all there with smiles on their faces. I'm reminded of the guy who once asked me, "How does it feel to have half a relationship formed with millions of people?" It feels good, very good, but it carries with it a certain responsibility. Clearly it's about M*A*S*H. We have in common a love for this show that became a social phenomenon and I'm happy to carry the banner for its message. But the embrace of it—and of me—the sense of personal relationship and appreciation, is almost overwhelming at times.

So I thank them for coming and talk a bit about the book, about my personal journeys and how my sense of social responsibility and the extraordinary luck I've had in my career intertwine, and then ask what questions they might have. This evening's group is again a mix of people with different concerns, but a couple of them stand out. A young woman is here after driving, as I have, from Tucson. Her mother, she says, was upset about missing me there, so she's here to get me to sign a book for her mother and one for her father and is then going to drive all the way back. A bit stunned at this, but happy to oblige, I wanted to write something about the extraordinary lengths she'd gone to, but she wouldn't let me. She said she didn't want them to know she'd come all the way down here because she thought they'd be mad. Despite my protests, she took the two books and left to make the drive back. Amazing!

Then there was a question about the hope of meeting Shelley, which allowed me to apologize and explain her absence. This is followed by a voice from the back of the crowd, a Latino man who asks with a grin, "Did you ever live in San Diego?" Seeing something in his eyes, I said, "Not since I joined the Marines and went through boot camp there." And he said, "I know, I was there with you." He came up and produced a photo I hadn't seen in fifty years, a group shot of all of us in Platoon 374 at MCRD, the Marine Corps Recruit Depot in San Diego. What an incredible hoot! After Arturo and I talked for a bit, the young woman from Tucson was back, saying she'd called her brother and he was mad because she didn't get a book for him, so she needed a third. And now, she said, she was "busted" because her folks knew about her jaunt, so she wanted a picture with me to be able to show them.

This crowd was wonderful. We laughed and talked about all kinds of things. But this life is hard, sometimes, to square with reality. People reach out in the most incredibly generous ways, wanting to say hello, to express gratitude for what the show meant to them, to know a little something about what I'm doing and why I do it. It is deeply touching and so very humbling.

People from the El Pasoans Against the Death Penalty cosponsored this event. A woman from an antipoverty organization came. Two doctors and a nurse brought their sons to meet me because of what *M*A*S*H* meant to them. A man asked about the political scene and if I'd be willing to say who I was supporting for president. I said I wasn't sure it would be appropriate to say my candidate's name, but I could say it was very prominent in the news and that it isn't McCain and it isn't Clinton.

DAY FOUR

Tuesday, May 13, 2008

CITY OF ORIGIN: EL PASO, TX   **CITY OF DESTINATION:** SANTA FE, NM

MILES TRAVELED: 328

TRAVEL DAY

An easy day, travel only. Mule and I just have to get to Santa Fe, New Mexico, for a bookstore event tomorrow night. Heading back into New Mexico on 10W, I decide to stop in Las Cruces and try to look up my old friend Blair, one of the guys from school who was in the club with Rick and me.

The wind is up again today and Las Cruces is covered with a cloud of brown dust. I call Blair hoping to see him for an hour or so, but get a machine. I leave a message explaining that I'm just passing through and hope to catch him, then drive around the city for a bit to see if he'll call back, eventually scouting out a health food store where I pick up lunch. After another call and still no Blair, we hightail it up Interstate 25 North toward Santa Fe where I'm invited to stay with Eugenie and Bobby, friends from Los Angeles who have a home north of town.

This is new territory for me, never having driven up through the center of New Mexico before, and I'd been warned by a woman in El Paso that it was "desolate." Sparsely populated, certainly, and flat as hell for a while, but the terrain is covered with scrub brush and doesn't seem any more desolate than the desert we've pushed through for the past few days. The wind keeps the dust flying and pushes Mule around a bit, but other than being attacked by the biggest tumbleweed I've ever seen there's nothing out of the ordinary. Mule behaves well as we climb gradually toward what look, through the dust, to be rolling hills.

Sean Hannity's nonsense helps pass the time as he exchanges what seems to be a new mantra with each caller: "You're a great American, Sean!" "You're a great American, Jack," or Bill, or Steve, or Zeke. (No, no Zekes.) The women callers seem to uniformly express how fearful they are at the possibility of an Obama presidency, while the men, after assuring each other they are "great Americans," complain to Sean about McCain's apostasy. It seems he has betrayed the movement by admitting that there may be something after all to this global warming business.

Between the "Stop Obama Express" and what now appears to be the "Get McCain Back on the Tracks" campaign, Sean's got a lot of work to do. But he's up to it, Great Americans. With righteousness in his heart and God on his side, he'll steer this country back to the legitimate Reagan-loving conservative cause. Sean is very strong in defense of the much-misunderstood George W. Bush, who will, "mark my words," be vindicated in the future; he'll go down in history as the president who protected us from terrorism, built up our defenses and put America back into a forward-leaning posture in the world.

Not only that, but in response to another Great American who described himself as a "charter member" of Rush's Operation Chaos, Hannity pays tribute to Limbaugh's genius (urging his dittoheads to cross over and vote for Hillary in the "Democrat" primaries to keep stirring the pot and create continuing havoc for them, maybe even to the point of causing "riots in the streets of Denver" during the "Democrat" convention), saying Chaos was the best thing he's ever done and claiming the strategy was responsible for Hillary Clinton's win in Indiana.

Having heard as much as I can stand, I hit the "off" button and pay attention to the alternating hills and arroyos we're crossing as we climb, noting in particular the wind- and water-scoured cliff faces that lead up to the now-more-numerous New Mexican mesas. Not desolate at all, but rather majestic testimony to the forces of nature and the passage of time.

As I near Albuquerque, Blair calls. He's sorry we missed each other, but he's been with his wife Sylvia in the hospital where she's being treated for an intestinal problem. She'll be okay, he's been assured, so we catch up a bit and promise to connect next time—hopefully at the reunion in July.

Once in Santa Fe I connect with Eugenie and Bobby. He meets me at a turnoff north of the city and leads me down a steep, twisting dirt road into the "hollow" where I'm quickly sheltered in the embrace of their fabulous adobe home.

DAY FIVE

Wednesday, May 14, 2008

CITY: SANTA FE, NM

VENUE: COLLECTED WORKS BOOKSTORE

SPECIAL GUESTS

Ambassador Joseph C. Wilson and Valerie Plame

T oday was a dream—the first part almost literally. After spending the evening catching up with Bobby and Eugenie—both are successful writer/producers in television and longtime friends who come to their gorgeous Santa Fe "getaway" as often as they can—I turn in kind of late, only to awaken with a start at the thought that I might have forgotten a radio interview scheduled for the first thing in the morning. Leaping out of bed to check the multipage itinerary (complete with names, dates, places, bookstores, hotels, motels, directions . . .), I find that I'm right. I'm to do a Santa Fe Public Radio interview at 8:30 in the morning and it's about 2 a.m. and I have no alarm clock and I don't want to wake Eugenie and Bobby and . . . Shit! What the hell do I do?

Okay, okay, don't panic. Just think! Well, there is one thing . . . Years ago I learned a trick: envision a big clock and carefully set the hands to the time you want to wake up and you'll wake up at that time. Uh-huh.

Well, hell, it won't hurt to try. But what if my body/mind is still on Pacific time? God . . . Anyway, I set the clock in my brain and just force myself to believe I'll wake up . . . maybe I'll have to pee. Something.

An hour or two later there's a hell of a rainstorm—maybe a hailstorm—whatever, it's loud and it wakes me. Great. Now it's 4 a.m. At this rate I'll either sleep till noon or be so groggy from lack of it that I'll be a flaming idiot on the radio . . .

My eyes pop open again! It's 5 a.m. This is torture. Open the curtains, maybe the light will wake me in spite of the clouds.

Argh! I'm awake! What time? It's 7:15. Amazing. It sort of worked. Or something worked. Stagger into a cold shower, throw on some clothes—forget about shaving, this is radio—and head to the car. The steep, winding gravel road I followed Bobby down last night looks very different from this angle. Still steep and winding, but there are turns I don't remember . . .

Finally, the highway; then the run into Santa Fe. The interview is to be done at the Santa Fe Baking Company, so I prowl the streets and finally find it. Looking around, I see a lot of people eating or having coffee, but no sign of a radio station.

A big, friendly guy seems to be running things, so I ask if I'm in the right place. "Sure," he says, and points to the corner of the room. "Mary-Charlotte is right over there." And right he is. Sitting in a corner of this bustling place is a pretty young woman, Mary-Charlotte Domandi, wearing a pair of headphones and talking to a man across from her who is also wearing headphones.

Turns out I'm early, so I order a smoothie and sit down. Mary-Charlotte looks up, sees me, waves, and goes back to her conversation.

Once it's my turn, the headphones on and the noise of this happy and popular restaurant blocked out, the interview is great. She's very bright, says she loves the book and, from the questions in the ensuing half-hour conversation, has clearly read it. In all, it's a delight. I'm sure glad I woke up.

I've often thought a job like hers would be fun. Meeting all kinds of different people speaking to all kinds of different issues from all kinds of perspectives has to be both challenging and exciting, not to mention enlightening.

Already in town, I decide to find the Collected Works Bookstore and nose around a bit. Nice people. It's one of those places that reeks of a love of books, making you feel good when you walk in the door.

After a walk around the plaza that gives me a sense of the place—the covered boardwalks and old adobe-style buildings transport you to another time—I head back out to Bobby and Eugenie's to clean up and get ready for the day.

Midday I call Joe. Joe Wilson, the former ambassador who blew the Bush administration out of the water by exposing W's now-infamous sixteen-word State of the Union lie—the claim that Saddam was trying to get yellowcake from Africa to make nuclear weapons—is a friend. Filmmaker Robert Greenwald and I first got in touch with him in the early pre–Iraq War days when we were organizing Artists United to Win Without War, and our relationship has grown ever since. Joe and his wife Valerie Plame Wilson, the once-covert CIA agent who was outed and had her career destroyed by the Bush-Cheney-Rove-Libby-etc. axis as payback for Joe's humiliating them, now live in Santa Fe, and Joe is to introduce me tonight at the bookstore.

He invites us over, so I get ready for the event, since I'll ride with Joe and Valerie to the bookstore later. Then Eugenie, Bobby and I head back to the city and up to the Wilsons' place, where the five of us sit and gab for an hour. Eugenie and Valerie have been in touch by phone and e-mail. Bobby has not met either of them, so it's a treat to bring them all together. The Wilsons are very impressive, quite wonderful hosts, and they are certainly, in the parlance of the day, a "power couple." But they're also very easy to be with and full of interesting experiences and views. Valerie, a gorgeous blonde, is so sweet and disarming it's sometimes hard to envision her in the life she describes (to the degree the CIA allowed her to do so) in her book. (The CIA's redactions in the book are outrageous, clearly an attempt to stifle her, so it was perfect that she had the journalist Laura Rozen fill in the blanks and make the government's ham-handed censors look stupid.) She spends a lot of time on the public-speaking circuit these days. Joe, still fit and looking very much the only-slightly-more-mature version of the Southern California surfer he was before launching a twenty-plus-year career in the diplomatic corps, is an eloquent and riveting speaker and remains very much in the struggle to change the political dynamic in this country. To top it all off, they are the actively devoted parents of a couple of kids, beautiful, spirited eight-year-old twins.

Joe has been a loyal supporter of Hillary Clinton's campaign and isn't yet ready to throw in the towel, remaining in the "anything can happen" mode, but he's realistic enough to be able to read the tea leaves. His primary concern is the election of a president who will commit to the reestablishment of the Constitution; he and Valerie are both willing to lend their considerable energies to seeing that happen.

Eugenie and Bobby take off. She's been preparing food all day (a great cook, she's creative and thoughtful, taking care to have plenty for a vegetarian—even a vegan!) and is getting set for all of us to have

AMBASSADOR JOSEPH C. WILSON

Over the past thirty-plus years that I have been involved in foreign policy and American politics, one of the most consequential changes I have experienced has been the growth of Nongovernmental Organizations (NGOs), Private Voluntary Organizations (PVOs), and political activist groups more generally. Their impact on political decisions and policy directions cannot be underestimated.

In my own career, I have seen the impact of these organizations on the deliberations of the U.S. government, on the passage of laws, and on the behavior of foreign governments. Throughout Africa, the International Foundation for Electoral Systems, the National Democratic Institute, and the International Republican Institute have spearheaded efforts to ensure transparency and integrity in the conduct of elections that have led to the opening of governments and the enhancement of democracy across the continent. The efforts of organizations such as Journalists Without Borders over a generation have succeeded in protecting journalists across the continent as well.

On the humanitarian front, I witnessed the efforts of NGOs to ensure that American assistance to Africa was maintained, and even enhanced, despite domestic budgetary pressures. It was American activists who were successful in persuading President Bush to tackle HIV/AIDS in Africa as a health issue, even as conservatives continued to see it as a "gay plague."

In my own personal life, political activist organizations have played key roles. When my wife's identity as a covert CIA officer was betrayed by her own government, it was an activist law group, Citizens for Responsibility and Ethics in Washington (CREW), that agreed to take our case, and to help us find some justice and hold the Bush administration to account for its despicable actions. That civil suit is winding its way through the appeals process; it is precedent setting. The question before our justice system is not whether some harm was done to the Wilson family, but rather, is it acceptable for government officials to engage in private political attacks from their positions of public trust? If they succeed in doing it to us with impunity, what is to prevent them from doing it to other citizens? Where is our privacy protection? We could not have pursued this suit on behalf of all American citizens, trying to safeguard our constitutional rights to privacy and of free speech, were it not for CREW.

I have also been personally involved in the efforts of the Military Religious Freedom Foundation, an organization dedicated to ensuring that all members of the United States Armed Forces receive the guarantee of religious freedom to which they and all Americans are entitled by virtue of the First Amendment. The organization currently represents hundreds of citizens who have suffered religious discrimination while in uniform, over ninety percent of whom are Christian.

Alexis de Toqueville noted a century and a half ago that the United States was a collection of special interests. We remain so. Until fairly recently, those interests that impacted on the policy making of governments were narrow in scope and often antithetical to broader interests. That has changed with the growth of activist groups who now successfully compete in the marketplace of ideas, guaranteeing that governments pay heed to voices other than those who formerly dominated the policy making process. It is a welcome change.

dinner at their place after the bookstore event. Bobby will meet us there, along with Gary, another writer and old friend who is their neighbor.

After more talk and some dealing with the kids, whom we leave happy in the capable hands of Heather—a former New York lawyer who gave it all up to come to Santa Fe to revive herself and is now the Wilson's nanny, assistant and woman-of-all-seasons—we head for Collected Works.

The event—standing room only—could hardly have been better. Joe's introduction is flattering beyond words and the interaction with the crowd is fun. Again, the discussion is wide-ranging—the war, the Bush administration, politics in general, the responsibility of citizenship, *M*A*S*H,* of course, the death penalty, criminal justice. One questioner raises a point I've heard something about: the New Mexico legislature was ready to abolish the death penalty and, as the story goes, Governor Richardson asked an ally to see that it didn't happen because he didn't want it brought to him for signature. What, the questioner asks, can we do? "Let him have it," I suggest. "He should hear from every one of you who cares about this issue. This is just plain political cowardice. We know he wanted to be president and he may still be angling to be on the ticket as vice president, and I understand that ambitious politicians fear being labeled as 'soft on crime,' but we need leaders who are willing to lead. Every thinking person knows the death penalty is rife with problems that are harming our society and those who want to take leadership positions have to have the guts to face up to the big issues and be leaders."

Later, when signing copies of my book, the man who asked the question introduced himself. He's Father John Dear, a highly respected Catholic priest who has written a number of books, mostly on peace and justice issues. I was delighted to meet him and thrilled that he cared enough to come tonight. I've worked with his brother, Steve Dear, who heads People of Faith Against the Death Penalty in North Carolina and have heard about John for years.

Afterward, we gathered at Bobby and Eugenie's for a wonderful dinner; the conversation, of course, centered on Joe and Valerie's experiences and their sense of things today. Joe had just returned from Saudi Arabia, where he, along with former government officials from a couple of NATO nations, met with very high-level Saudis. He said they were not impressed with their relationship with the current U.S. administration, which does a lot of "telling" and very little listening. The message Dick Cheney delivered back to Washington after his recent visit, they said, was not at all what they had conveyed to him. In fact, it was so wrong that they had to resort to sending an emissary to correct him and make sure the proper message got through. However, even once delivered, whether it actually "got through" is in question.

Everyone, Joe says, is concerned that all the Bush administration's choices and actions are only further inflaming the Middle East, further empowering Iran, and making things worse for those trying to find a way toward peace. Everyone believes that the U.S. should be engaging Iran in talks—treating them with the respect due any sovereign nation—rather than continuing to ratchet up tensions between our country and theirs.

A fascinating discussion. I hated to have it end, but Valerie had to catch a plane the next day and, oh yeah, I have to get up early to drive to Taos for a radio interview . . .

DAY SIX

Thursday, May 15, 2008

CITY OF ORIGIN: SANTA FE, NM

MILES TRAVELED: 70

CITY OF DESTINATION: TAOS, NM

VENUE: HARWOOD MUSEUM OF ART

EVENT COSPONSORS

Society of the Muse of the Southwest, UNM-Taos Library

Bobby, who evidently rises early every day, was my alarm clock this morning. He knocked at a few minutes before 7 a.m. and I was ready and out the door before 8, complete with a goody bag from Eugenie, who insisted that I eat this morning.

It's raining, so I wanted to have enough time to get to the radio station for the 9:30 a.m. interview on KTAO, known as "K-TAOS, the world's only solar-powered radio station."

Driving north through the rain I reflect a bit on one of the things Joe Wilson told us about yesterday. He's on the board of Mikey Weinstein's Military Religious Freedom Foundation, and had recently visited the Air Force Academy with him. Weinstein, Academy graduate, Air Force lawyer and former counsel in the Reagan White House, had been offended by anti-Semitic slurs against his Air Force–cadet son and founded the MRFF to counter the increasing fundamentalist Christian proselytizing he found when taking a look at the situation in the Academy.

In that pursuit, he told BuzzFlash.com, "What I found at the Air Force Academy was nothing short of something that could destroy the republic. An essentially evangelical, fundamentalist, Christian perspective was being imposed on those that were not evangelical fundamentalist Christians, in complete and total disregard of the First Amendment and the Bill of Rights, where the separation of church and state clearly resides."

As part of a growing campaign on the part of the MRFF to shine a light on this problem, he and Joe went to the Academy to speak to the cadets and wanted to show, as part of their presentation, the trailer of a new documentary, *Constantine's Sword,* that puts in context and exposes the degree of Christian evangelical pressure now being placed, by their superior officers, on Air Force cadets. The officer in charge of the institution, however, objected to their showing the footage. Joe and Weinstein argued that the trailer of their film, only twelve minutes long, could hardly do any damage, especially since Mel Gibson's film *The Passion of the Christ,* filled with what are seen by some as stereotypical and biased depictions of Jews and their relationship to the crucifixion of Jesus, had been widely shown there, as well as a video made by a group called Christian Embassy that featured Air Force Major General Jack Catton Jr., Army Brigadier General Vince Brooks (former public affairs director of the Army), and Undersecretary of the Army Peter Geren openly promoting their religious views. Nonetheless, Joe said, although they were allowed to speak, they could not show their trailer due to what was clearly pressure from above.

This kind of proselytizing, Joe said, is going on not only at the Air Force Academy but is deeply rooted in all the military academies and presents a growing problem that manifests itself as the politicization of the military. The religious view promoted is not only anti-Semitic, it is anti-Catholic, anti–mainstream Protestant and, in essence, wants to root out any belief that is not the kind of dominionist, fundamentalist, evangelical Christian view promoted by Pat Robertson and the late Jerry Falwell.

Scary stuff. A good man, Joe Wilson, doing good work on many fronts.

The rain lightens up a bit as I move further north. Mule is handling the water well and we're getting along just fine.

The land here is impressive; whether sculpted by ancient glaciers or wind and water—possibly all three—the earth takes on arresting shapes: mounds, mesas with steep, sharp sides rest next to deep arroyos, and large, oddly shaped mountains with names like Camel Rock and Elephant Rock. The earth forms, plus some names reflecting early Native American and later Spanish settlement give the land a somewhat magical feeling, earning it the title Land of Enchantment.

About halfway to Taos, Mule and I enter a deep, beautiful canyon that's been cut into the New Mexican highland by the Rio Grande. After making our way through the canyon for some miles, we climb out to the top of the highland as the canyon falls away off to the left, wending its way north and west.

Taos is a lovely little place, kind of a miniature Santa Fe. The traditional adobe structures are everywhere here, with their flat roofs, thick walls and rounded, molded corners. I remember, when first entering Bobby and Eugenie's home, feeling that the thickness of the walls and graceful, round softness of every corner gave it a feeling of voluptuousness. They've made theirs a work of art, but the sense of strength given off by all of these old adobes says a lot about their place in history.

Evidently, Kit Carson made his home here in Taos.

Not sure where I'll find the radio station, I end up going all the way through town and out the other end without seeing the turnoff described in my directions, so I call to find out if I've gone too far. "Nope," I'm told, "you're doing fine. Keep going." It turns out the station is well out beyond the northern edge of the city.

Nancy Stapp, the host of *Breakfast with Nancy,* reminds me that she interviewed me some time back when she was with the Air America radio network out of Eugene, Oregon. They've all been planning to meet Shelley too, and even played "Johnny Angel" as part of my introduction, so once again I have to apologize and explain why my wife wasn't able to join me on the book tour. (When playing Mary Stone on *The Donna Reed Show*, Shelley's recording of the song stayed at the top of the charts for weeks in 1962, becoming the theme song for a generation of young lovers that, men and women remind me constantly, stirs them to this day. The women all wanted to *be* Shelley, the men all fell in love with her.)

> ### SOMOS (SOCIETY OF THE MUSE OF THE SOUTHWEST)
>
> Somos, founded in 1983, supports and nurtures the literary arts, in both written and oral traditions, honoring cultural diversity in the Southwest.
>
> Somos was formed as an organization to provide an arena for writers of all mediums to read and perform their work. Early on, Somos brought award-winning author Sam Oeur to Taos. Oeur's work commemorates and memorializes the innocent dead of collective fascism. Many other courageous authors have passed through Taos in the intervening years.
>
> The organization's advisory board includes Marjorie Agosin; Jimmy Santiago Baca, an acclaimed Native Hispanic poet; James Nave, an alum of Poetry Alive; noted Latino author and historian Rudolpho Anaya; and John Nichols, author of *The Milagro Beanfield War.*

The interview is relaxed and fun. It's great to talk to people who have actually read my book and can discuss aspects of it rather than simply asking me what it's about. Nancy is very kind, paying a lovely compliment by saying that when reading the book she felt as though I was talking directly to her.

Once the show is over I have some time to kill before the event, so I head for the library where I can catch up on e-mail and current events. I'm stunned to read that this miserable, wretched excuse for a national leader, the pathetic, smirking narcissist who occupies our White House, has taken the opportunity to turn an address to the Israeli Knesset into a political attack on Barack Obama's stated willingness to speak to those who oppose us and our allies. Forget that Reagan talked to Gorbachev, that Nixon met with Mao, that JFK dealt with Krushchev, let's cheapen an ostensibly respectful visit to Israel on its sixtieth anniversary by, of all tasteful things, raising the specter of the Nazis and implying that Obama is somehow talking about dancing with terrorists.

What an utterly cheap, completely chickenshit stunt. Joe Biden was absolutely right to drop the usual careful Washingtonese protocol and tell it like it is: "Bullshit!"

Cooling off with a bite to eat, I then make my way to the event at the Harwood Museum of Art. But first I have to find the Harwood Museum of Art, which is not as easy as one would think, especially given the

---

Somos continues to bring writers together to share their work with the public through summer and winter readings, workshops, and seminars. The participating authors are published in *Chokecherries*, a yearly publication of the poets and writers, photographers and painters who make up the collective spirit of Somos. The organization shares the creative spirit with the youth of Taos through a Youth Mentorship Program, in which experienced writers are paired with students who are then published in *Cross Polination*, another annual publication. In addition, Somos brings the Storytelling Festival to Taos every fall with the best national storytellers presenting their work before large crowds. Tania Cassell, the noted Scottish writer, puts Somos on the air with a weekly radio program.

We at Somos believe that expression brings about awareness and gives voice to the value that truth is of supreme importance.

size of this town. Finally, after circling and searching, I have the presence of mind to stop and ask someone, and voilà! Down a narrow—and frighteningly deserted—one-way street, I finally zero in on the Harwood. Pulling into the small parking lot in front, my growing sense of foreboding is heightened by the fact that there's only one other car visible. A young man, Bobby Arellano, actually another Akashic Books author who teaches at the University of New Mexico and is the person who has organized this event, comes out to greet me. He's very pleasant and doesn't appear to be as stricken as I would expect him to be if no one had actually showed up, so I take heart and walk into the building with him. There are two people leaving, another not-good sign, but the woman, who is kind and apologizes for not being able to stay, holds out a copy of the book and asks if I'd mind signing it anyway. Why not? It might be the only one.

Inside, three or four people are standing at a table, registering for something. Bobby introduces me and then we walk down a hall and up a flight of stairs—an extremely quiet flight of stairs. I'm developing the sinking feeling that, despite his very pleasant manner, Bobby is trying to figure out how to break it to me that everyone seems to have had something else to do tonight . . . then we round a corner and enter a room where about fifty people are sitting, apparently waiting for little old me.

God, what a relief.

As it happens, we're a bit early and others are actually coming in behind us, so Bobby lets me roam for a while and appreciate the work displayed while the audience gathers. Taos is quite the art community and the Harwood is apparently a very successful and highly regarded museum. What I have time to see are some very old—and evidently very precious—religious paintings on wood, some of them quite primitive in appearance, and, in the room where the crowd is gathering, an impressive display of four contemporary Impressionists. (At least I think they're Impressionists. My knowledge of art is, shall we say, limited.)

As I'm looking around, a number of people come up and thank me for visiting Taos. It appears that there is a great sense of community pride here, and perhaps a bit of a sense that the city is not as fully appreciated as it might be. I'm not sure about that part, but whatever the case, the gratitude on their part for my coming is so clearly genuine that it is quite touching.

One man stands looking at me and asks, "Do you remember me?" I truly hate that question—unless, of course, I do remember—because it inevitably provides for an embarrassing moment for one or both of us. "From where should I remember you?" I ask. "Anicam," he says. Anicam was an animation camera service my brother worked at many years ago, and this man, it turns out, is the son of the founder of the company. "Of course," I say, happy to have the point of reference. "I'll tell Jim I saw you."

By the time Bobby signals me in to be introduced, there must be a couple hundred people in the room, which almost makes me laugh out loud from further relief. And the warmth, attention and sense of appreciation that flows out at me from the moment of his introduction is staggering. The evening could not have been better, nor could I have been made to feel more at home.

Driving back down to Bobby and Eugenie's for the night, I check in with Shelley, who is doing wonderfully. Though sore from the physical therapy, she's very happy with the progress she's making, as is the therapist. And once again I get to tell her that the very first question asked this evening was, "Where's Shelley?" It was from a man who wanted to thank her. He said he had played "Johnny Angel" over and over for the guys in his unit when he was in Vietnam in the late 1960s and he wanted to tell her how much it meant to all of them.

I thanked him on her behalf and said I'd make sure she got the message that very night.

DAY SEVEN
Friday, May 16, 2008

CITY OF ORIGIN: SANTA FE, NM   **CITY OF DESTINATION:** SONORA, TX

MILES TRAVELED: 619

TRAVEL DAY

U p early again. Have to cover a lot of distance today and there's a telephone interview to do first, this with a woman at the *Iowa Press-Citizen,* in anticipation of my arrival there (weeks from now, I assume).

The next gig is in Austin, Texas, almost 800 miles away, so I won't plan to get there tonight, but want to take a good bite out of it in order to get into the city relatively early tomorrow. I've not been to Austin and am looking forward to it. I keep hearing that it's the "Berkeley of Texas," a bastion of liberalism in an otherwise conservative state.

With thanks to Bobby and Eugenie for their gracious hospitality I head back into Santa Fe, through the narrow lanes of that lovely town, and finally to U.S. Highway 285, which runs a pretty straight shot southeast to West Texas.

It's beautiful heading down out of the highlands under a bright blue sky pebbled with cottony white clouds. Driving up from El Paso on Tuesday, the climb from Las Cruces to Santa Fe was so gradual as to not be obvious, but a climb it was. Like El Paso, Las Cruces is less than 4,000 feet above sea level (actually higher than I had thought), while Santa Fe is nearly 7,500, so Mule had work to do—and did it without complaint. It was a "beepless" day, thank heaven, without great panicky moments.

I filled up the tank in Taos last night despite the fact that I still had two squares showing on the gas gauge and could probably have easily made the sixty-five miles back down to Santa Fe, but since it was very dark and there wasn't a lot of civilization until we got close to Bobby and Eugenie's, I decided not to test Mule. And again this morning the gauge says it's still full.

As we race southward the mesas become less prominent and the land flattens out. It's interesting to watch the outside temperature rise (the one thing I *can* understand on the dash screen so full of complex diagrams and information) as our altitude falls. From the time we left Los Angeles and hit the desert, the outside temperature has been in the high nineties, only dropping into the high eighties in El Paso. Once we pushed up to Santa Fe it got into the sixties and fifties, dropping one morning into the forties, so having the connection between altitude and temperature spelled out before me is interesting. Taking full advantage of the downward slope and a lack of traffic, I push Mule along at a good clip. I figure I've now broken the speed laws in every state we've touched so far.

I'm still pissed at President Stupid. Actually, that's too easy. I've never been convinced he's the moron so many think he is. He seems to me to be quite clever in many ways, only one of them having manipulated himself into the spot he now occupies. Senator John Kerry once told me that he didn't think W. was at all stupid, but that he seemed to lack any intellectual curiosity. Once he determined that something was what he believed it to be, there was no questioning, no analysis and no willingness to budge. It's the position of a frightened child—or an utter narcissist. (How's this. I looked up Narcissistic Personality Disorder: *A pervasive pattern of grandiosity, need for admiration, and a lack of empathy.*)

As governor of Texas he presided over 152 executions and went so far as to mock the plea of one of them, Karla Faye Tucker, to a reporter. In Iraq, he's been responsible for over 4,000 U.S. military deaths, tens of thousands of injuries among our military personnel and perhaps hundreds of thousands of Iraqi civilian deaths. Has there been any sign of empathy?

That smirk makes me nuts.

But forget him for the moment. Here we are in southeastern New Mexico, zipping along under the now-less-cloudy blue sky. The flat, scrub-covered land stretches as far as one can see on each side, and when I look to the left I note the entrance to a vast, fenced piece of property with a sign over the gate that reads, *Victor Perez Ranch*. When I say vast, I mean that the road under the gate runs straight away from the highway and disappears over the horizon without a single structure in sight. Somewhere off in the far distance beyond the edge of the earth I envision a huge, elaborate ranch house and attendant structures looking like something out of the movie *Giant*.

Considering this as we roll along gets me thinking about the whole idea of owning property. As a city boy from a working-class background, I know the satisfaction that comes from owning a home and a piece of property, but thinking of Victor Perez and his rancho, or people like the characters in *Giant*, or so many others with huge landholdings—the kind of acreage that makes one understand the use of the word "spread"— gives me pause. It brings to mind the Native American concept of living in harmony with the land, perhaps as a visitor, or as one who is granted a kind of stewardship over it because it cannot be owned, as such; one lives in partnership with it.

Closing in on the Texas border we pass through the New Mexican town of Encino. Unlike the wealthy San Fernando Valley community of the same name, this Encino (meaning evergreen or a kind of oak tree) is a shambles. A virtual ghost town, to say it has fallen on hard times is to understate it by miles. Shuttered stores, overgrown yards, huge weeds covering the front of what was once a filling station mark some kind of tragedy in the lives of the people who once resided here—and the few who perhaps still do. Very sad to see this; shocking, in a way. And, not to make Victor Perez out to be a villain, because he's probably a nice man who worked hard for what he has, the disparity between some lives and others in this country is writ large for me in these two sets of circumstances.

Crossing into Texas the clouds have come together and turned gray. Soon there is a steady sprinkle on us that continues down to and through the town of Pecos, *Home of the World's First Rodeo*, per the signs. And as we cross the Pecos River I note that Mule and I are no longer "west of the Pecos."

Rattling on down, I see that we again have two squares left on the gas gauge. Fort Stockton, where we'll hook up again with Interstate 10E, is about fifty-five miles away, so instead of stopping to fill up I figure we'll just sniff haughtily at the gas stations and keep right on going.

And we do.

Less than an hour later, as my attention is diverted to making the correct turn to get onto the interstate, Mule hesitates and seems to lose power. Suddenly I'm hearing all kinds of beeps!

"What the hell . . . ?"

"Mule can't run with no oats."

"What? But we had two full squares!"

"Look again, smart guy. There's only one now and it's blinkin'. And that red triangle with the exclamation point in it? That's not a good thing."

Shit, the one remaining square is blinking its head off, there are red lights flashing on the dash and the damned car is beeping and slowing down.

"Damnit, Mule, you can't do this! Don't quit on me now! Not here, we're in the middle of the goddamned highway!"

"Not up to me. You're the hero who wants to see how far you can go. Take a good look; this is it."

"No, come on! You're electric, what about that? Can't you run on the battery?"

"Whaddya think I been doin'? See that thing in the middle of the screen, the one says *Battery*? It's s'posed to have four or five of them little blue lines across it; see how many it's got?"

There were two—and one was fading fast. We're putting along, ever more slowly, but at least there aren't any cars racing up behind us.

"Can't I charge it? Doesn't it charge when I put on the brakes?"

"You sure you want to do that, Sherlock?"

"No, no! Of course not! But if I take my foot off the gas?"

"You're the boss, boss."

We're literally creeping along. When I take my foot off the accelerator the remaining blue line seems to brighten a bit, but it also makes us go slower—and if we go any slower . . .

"Jesus, Mule, there's a turnoff up ahead. Don't quit on me now."

"I'm losing my voice here . . ."

All kinds of scenarios are playing out in my head: pull off and hitch a ride to get some gas; push the damned car off the interstate; flag someone down and explain . . . that I thought . . . well, see, these things don't use much gas . . . Uh-huh, yes. Evidently they do need *some* once in a while.

But we roll forward and just make it to the turnoff. We're down under ten miles an hour and I see, off on the other side of the interstate, a sign for a gas station.

"Mule, look! Over there! Come on, pal, we can make it!"

"Don't call me pal," he wheezes.

Amazingly, we creep into the station and up to the pump. Just as I hit the brake, everything goes dead. Sweating and shaking with relief, I get out of the car and grab the pump. As the gas pours into the empty tank I think I hear a faint whisper—"Asshole!"

Gassed up and all paid for—and just to get back on her good side I wash the windshield—I'm not sure what to expect, but cross my fingers, put my foot on the brake and push the *Power* button. God bless her, she starts up—no bells, no whistles, no mumbled imprecations. Maybe, I think, all is forgiven.

Back on the 10E things look pretty good. Texas is greener down here than I remembered and the etched walls and mesas to the north are very pretty. One has been eaten away to the degree that it looks like a pyramid—with a little pillbox hat on top. The speed limit on the interstate down here in West Texas is eighty mph, a number I don't remember seeing anywhere else.

Mule doesn't seem to mind it, so we press on. But I do need to check in somewhere with a TV so I can watch the Lakers/Jazz game. They're playing in Utah, which can be tough, but the Lakers really need to put these guys away. Sonora, Texas looks good. It's a ways down the line yet, but if I can get there and grab a bite to eat before the game I should be okay. That'll leave us about a three-hour trip to make it to Austin tomorrow.

Right, Mule?

Mule?

DAY EIGHT
Saturday, May 17, 2008

CITY OF ORIGIN: SONORA, TX

MILES TRAVELED: 195

CITY OF DESTINATION: AUSTIN, TX

VENUE: BOOKPEOPLE

EVENT COSPONSOR
Texas Coalition to Abolish the Death Penalty

T he first thing I do this morning is look out the peephole in the door to see if Mule is still there. She is, thank God. Hasn't spoken to me since that . . . slight mishap . . . and I wasn't sure she wouldn't steal off in the night. I didn't get a lot of sleep worrying about her. I apologized all over the place and promised that I'd never let the gas gauge get down below two squares again, but she still wouldn't talk. I'm hoping the fact that she's still out there means we're okay again.

Anyway, we made it to Sonora for the Lakers/Jazz game last night. We're on Central time now, so it didn't start until 9:30 here and I think it was after midnight before it was over. I'll bet Utah wishes it had lasted even later as they were on a scary roll in the last few seconds, but time ran out and the Lakers won. Next it's the Spurs or the Hornets.

Mule starts up without a snort and we head out into the rain again, but the rolling hills are green and pretty and she perks right along, so

I'm feeling pretty good. Rather than going down to San Antonio and then north, we cut off 10E onto Highway 290 and make a beeline for Austin through the Texas Hill Country. I have to say I'm impressed. I've been through it a number of times and I always expect Texas to be hot and dry and flat and brown. And it is, in parts, but this area is beautiful. The rain stops and it stays fairly cool as we cruise along between great groves of gorgeous, thick green trees separated by the occasional goat or horse ranch. I haven't seen any cattle for quite awhile.

Crossing the Pedernales River (which Texans seem to want to pronounce PER-din-AH-less) I begin to suspect we're in LBJ country. And we are, it becomes clear, as we pass through Fredericksburg, which boasts the Lady Bird Johnson Park, and then Johnson City, where LBJ was born. Fredericksburg is a beautiful city, clean and well-kept, with street signs and store names indicating a German influence. Lots of tourists. Johnson City, on the other hand, boasts of the former president at every opportunity, but looks a bit the worse for wear.

Austin is a big place, bigger somehow than I had expected. Checking into the hotel, I just have time for a quick change and then head out to a reception arranged by the Texas Coalition to Abolish the Death Penalty at a lovely private home not too far from the University of Texas. A warm and friendly group is gathered, some of whom I met when I spoke at the TCADP conference in Houston in January. This is a courageous bunch, taking on the death penalty in the most kill-happy state in the union, but they're dedicated, hard at work and making progress.

The district attorney in Harris County, the most killing county in this most killing state, was recently run out of office in a scandal caused by the release, in court, of hundreds of e-mails he had sent from his office computer that exposed him as a womanizer, a cheater, and a racist. They're good at looking the other way, but even the good ol' boys couldn't ignore all that. To top it off, the Houston crime lab has been mired in a scandal of its own, with the discovery of hundreds of boxes of "misplaced" evidence concerning 8,000 cases dating from over thirty years ago.

Police are investigating(!).

And in Dallas, a new district attorney is cooperating with a process of DNA testing for potential innocence in a number of old cases in that jurisdiction, which has resulted in eighteen exonerations and caused an uproar that is having statewide ramifications.

Also, the *Dallas Morning News,* after years of unquestioning support for state killing, published a series of editorials investigating the subject and has now called for an end to capital punishment in Texas.

So, these good, if beleaguered, folks at TCADP, who are doing everything they can to break their fellow Texans of this "cultural" bias toward the death penalty, are making strides and deserve all the support we can provide them.

From the reception, Bob, a retired military officer and one of the leaders of TCADP, leads me to the BookPeople bookstore, right near the

TEXAS COALITION TO ABOLISH THE DEATH PENALTY

The Texas Coalition to Abolish the Death Penalty (TCADP) is a grassroots, statewide organization composed of human rights activists, murder victims' family members, death row inmates and their families, academics, attorneys, people of faith, civic and civil rights leaders, and concerned citizens. Founded in 1995 in Houston by a small group of volunteers, TCADP now has twelve local chapters, a central office in Austin, and thousands of members and supporters statewide.

While abolishing the death penalty in Texas is an uphill battle (to say the least!), TCADP's efforts to educate Texans about the flaws and failures of the capital punishment system have gained tremendous ground in recent years. Ongoing organizational activities include a religious outreach program, an annual conference, execution vigils, and film screenings.

In 2008, TCADP launched a victims' outreach program, in order to lift up the voices of those di-

university (and right across from the home base of Whole Foods), for tonight's book event.

A very nice crowd of terrific folks are there and we have a good time. Before the event, a career Army man, leader of a Green Beret team, pulled me aside and said how much *M*A*S*H* has meant to him and his family, who are all there to hear me. He's still in the Army, his wife is an Army nurse and their son is serving in Iraq. His daughter, still in college, is considering breaking ranks and becoming a veterinarian. Nice folks. Then another man cornered me; he's close to Magdaleno Rose-Avila, a good friend of mine and one of the premier voices for social justice in the country.

The presentation goes very well, with lots of questions about all the issues—and about *M*A*S*H*, of course—and at the end I introduce Bob, who will pass out brochures and happily answer any questions about TCADP, which is cosponsoring this evening's talk.

People line up to have me sign books, which is the routine. When I get to the end of this line, however, a tall, good-looking young man with dark hair hands me a book. When I ask his name, he says, "It's

rectly impacted by this issue, and it has been at the forefront of efforts to raise awareness of the intersection between the death penalty and severe mental illness. In addition, TCADP recently concluded a year-long concert series entitled "Music for Life," which featured Austin-based singer/songwriter Sara Hickman. Sara performed in a different Texas city each month, where her concerts provided a forum for dialogue about the death penalty and enhanced the visibility of the abolition movement.

TCADP has embarked on an ambitious five-year strategic plan aimed at achieving real legislative change in Texas. We invite all concerned citizens to become members of TCADP. Residents of Texas can participate in the activities of their local chapter or host a program on the death penalty with their faith community, civic group, or student organization.

TCADP is honored to call Mike Farrell a friend and was pleased to host him twice in 2008. His visits, and his long-standing commitment to ending the death penalty, have provided inspiration and encouragement to TCADP members throughout the state to continue working for social change.

John. I think we're kind of related." "Really," I respond, "what's your last name?" "It's John Flynn," he says. "No kidding? Are you Joanne's son?" "Yes," he says, pointing to a lovely blond woman who has been sitting in the front row for the whole event, "she's right here."

It's amazing! This trip has really brought people out of the woodwork, but this is stunning. My father's youngest brother, an Army Air Corps officer, was killed in an automobile accident shortly before the end of World War II and left behind his wife and baby daughter Joanne. Gracie, his wife, left California and our families lost touch. About thirty years or so ago, my cousin Joanne came to Los Angeles and contacted me and we met and visited for a while. She then left for Houston and we somehow lost contact again. I had tried to find her, but to no avail. And here she is, three decades later.

Unbelievable! Bob has made plans to take me to dinner at a natural food restaurant, so when Joanne asks if I'll go somewhere with them, I tell her of our plans and invite the two of them to join us. It turns out that she not only knows the restaurant, but is close to the owner, so we all go out to dinner and reconnect. And this time we won't lose touch.

Life, huh?

DAY NINE

Sunday, May 18, 2008

CITY OF ORIGIN: AUSTIN, TX

MILES TRAVELED: 162

CITY OF DESTINATION: HOUSTON, TX

VENUE: BRAZOS BOOKSTORE

EVENT COSPONSOR
Texas Coalition to Abolish the Death Penalty

After sending an e-mail to my brother and sister about finding Joanne, I load up Mule and we head east to Houston. Rolling down the highway, I decide it's time for a little self-punishment, so I turn on the radio and am treated to a lecture from Focus on the Family about the danger to America that will result from the California Supreme Court's decision overturning the law against same-sex marriage. If allowed to stand, it's a disaster, I'm told, of cataclysmic proportions. I must say, though, that the legal expert who the host brings in to speak to the question does so in relatively sane tones, parsing and analyzing the decision relatively fairly. I mean, he clearly disagreed with it and feels that the decision is somehow a threat to right-thinking Christians, but I was impressed with the reasonable tone he brought to his analysis.

Then a news break informs me that our fearless leader decided to lecture the Arab world before heading home. He told them, the announcer says, in no uncertain terms, that they must release all political prisoners and allow for free, democratic elections. I wonder, as I'm hearing this galling pronouncement, if anyone bothered to ask him to do the same thing? What are the people in Guantánamo who have had no charges filed against them, if not political prisoners? What was the 2000 election in Florida, if not an insult to the idea of "free, democratic elections"? What about the free election that put Hamas in power in Gaza that the U.S. refuses to acknowledge? What an incredible—and embarrassing—fool the man is!

After an unsuccessful search in three stores for an apple or a banana, I'm back to the radio. Now a different guy is telling me that the California decision is a triumph for the "homosexual lobby" and it may just force "believing Christians" to ask themselves this question: "Do you support God or do you support your country?"

It's a powerful force, this homosexual lobby, he says, and though he doesn't want to get into spreading rumors, we all know about Arnold Schwarzenegger and his homosexual friends . . .

He actually said that. Then this guy continues, saying to his listeners that we might just find ourselves having to make a choice. They are going to put us in a situation where "obeying the law could put us in jeopardy with God."

This guy is a beaut. Later, when asked by a caller what "we" can do, he says (after demurring, saying he's not telling others what to do, but if it was up to him . . .), "All incumbents should be booted out." (Actually, if they're all in Texas, I kind of hope they take his advice.) He goes on to say that "Clinton, Obama and McCain are the embodiment of evil!"

Ladies and gentlemen, I kid you not.

I get to Houston and find the hotel, change and head out to an after-

noon book gig, this one again cosponsored by TCADP at an independent outfit called the Brazos Bookstore. (Though I have done and will in
the future do events at chains like Barnes & Noble, the folks at Akashic
Books are very interested in supporting independent bookstores.) Brazos was here, the new proprietor tells me, for over twenty years until
the owner decided to sell out two years ago. Unwilling to lose it, twenty-
eight people in the neighborhood came together and put up the money
to buy the store and keep it going.

Again, a lively discussion about good issues with thoughtful people.
Then Dave, one of the founders of TCADP, his wife, and three people
who do a lot of volunteer work with the group take me out to dinner.

And I get to turn in early before heading out to New Orleans tomorrow.

DAY TEN

Monday, May 19, 2008

CITY OF ORIGIN: HOUSTON, TX   **CITY OF DESTINATION:** NEW ORLEANS, LA

MILES TRAVELED: 348

TRAVEL DAY

Another day, another city, another state—and another . . . hiccup . . . but I'm getting ahead of myself.

Up and out of the hotel early for an interview for a local PBS station here. Not knowing Houston very well, I leave early because I want to allow plenty of time to get there. Every time I've been through here the traffic has been horrible. And it isn't wonderful this morning, but I manage to get to the University of Houston, where they shoot, in plenty of time.

Ernie Manouse, the interviewer, is very bright, quite personable, and he has done his homework, so the conversation—and it is just that—is easy and fun. For some reason I thought it was going to be a radio interview, so I didn't shave, but I guess if it's noticeable at all it gives me that cool Hollywood look that so many affect today.

Afterward, back on good old 10E toward New Orleans, I turn on the radio for another exercise in frustration. And I get it. I pick up a local

New Orleans talk show host who's interviewing people about the energy crunch and making me grind my teeth in the process. He has on a series of "experts" who think the solution to our dependency on foreign oil is to drill in ANWR, the Arctic National Wildlife Refuge, and to build more nuclear power plants. Drilling in ANWR will spoil one of the last and most critically irreplaceable wilderness areas and wildlife preserves in North America. It will also take years to realize any serious oil production from the area, and if we do, it is only estimated to hold enough oil to provide what is essentially a drop in the bucket in terms of U.S. consumption. As far as nuclear power is concerned, it has always seemed to me a lunatic notion to rely for energy on a process that creates waste that is lethal to human life for 250,000 years, with no safe way to dispose of it.

None of these geniuses mention conservation, which is said to have the ability to cut our energy consumption by a significant degree in and of itself, nor did they talk about solar, wind, geothermal or any of the other alternative methods available. Though it's clear that none of these are at this point far enough advanced to do the job themselves, together they can make a huge dent in our consumption of fossil fuel and wean us, to a large degree, from our oil dependency.

It's startling to hear these people casually suggest that the problem is with "the lawyers" in Washington and with all these bothersome restrictions laid on by the Environmental Protection Agency. All we have to do, to hear them say it, is blow off the clean air standards we've fought so hard to get implemented and let the oil companies drown us in their garbage while they continue to reap huge profits.

Sick of listening to this bilge, I turn to another station and hear a guy who's sitting in for Rush Limbaugh (who's probably at home sticking pins into Obama dolls) rage on about the "global warming hoax." It's a lie, it's a trick, they're trying to take away our right to our way of life!

Astonishing. I truly worry about the people who listen to this crap all the time.

Searching for something to soothe my fevered brow, I find an NPR station in which a woman is having a conversation, both verbally and musically, with Oscar Peterson. They talk for a while and then one or the other plays something on the piano, and then they talk again and then play again. It is really a treat.

And when that's over, the BBC comes on. Spending a few minutes listening to real newspeople reporting real news is enough to make one want to run the poseurs, pundits, panderers, proselytizers, pompous pronouncers, and product pimps out of their plush positions.

The BBC reports on a company that has developed—or perhaps redeveloped—a technology that produces electricity through a wind-up mechanism that they've made work for a radio. The idea is that in much of the underdeveloped world there is insufficient electricity—or no electricity at all—to operate radios and other such devices. A small, inexpensive thing like this can make a huge difference in the lives of people who are otherwise cut off from communicating with the rest of the world. They're also making it work with a lamp. And he mentions the fact that this process will eliminate the need for batteries, which are not only expensive for people in the underdeveloped world, but the disposal of which becomes a huge toxic waste problem. And these folks are doing all this through a not-for-profit organization!

It is so easy to do good in the world . . . Sometimes the blindness of people intent only on getting rich makes you want to weep.

Crossing into southeastern Louisiana, I stop in Lake Charles, find a health food store and then drive a ways off the highway to eat lunch in a quiet place. The next leg of the trip, starting about fifty miles into Louisiana and stretching all the way to Baton Rouge, just knocks me out. The Atchafalaya Basin is the largest swamp in the U.S., and the engineering feat necessary to build the "bridge," or elevated highway, that stretches across it, simply amazes me. The "bridge" (I guess it has to be considered that) runs for miles, probably twenty or more to cross the Atchafalaya, and is basically a highway set up on huge pillars that allows traffic to pass over this unbelievable expanse of bayous, cypress swamps, thick, apparently impenetrable forests, rivers, deltas, swamp grass, lakes and wetlands that stretches northward about 150 miles from the Gulf of Mexico. It's wild and mysterious and beautiful and largely uninhabited, and when I think about the work that had to go into building this road standing above it, it bends my mind.

People had to dig down into the swampy water and gouge out bases for the pillars, they had to set the pillars and lay the beams and the cement thirty feet or so above it all, and they had to do it when they were literally up to their asses in alligators and water moccasins and every kind of swimming, creeping and flying creature imaginable. For miles!

Despite the fact that it disturbed nature, and I think I'm fairly sensitive to that, I just find the creation of this structure to be a colossal, actually heroic feat. I'd love to read about the construction of the road.

I must have been over it before, but I first became truly aware of the miracle of it only six or seven years ago when my son Mike made this drive with me. I'd been asked by Greenpeace to take part in a tour they were arranging of what is known as Cancer Alley, a swatch of land between Baton Rouge and New Orleans, situated between the Mississippi

River on the west and Interstate 10 on the east. Laced with small communities of mostly black and poor white people, it is dotted with oil and chemical refineries and attendant industries that spill crap into the ground, the water, and the air. It became known as Cancer Alley because of the outrageous amount of disease that cropped up among the people who lived in the midst of this assault. (If curious, take a look at www.mikefarrell.org/publications/cancer.html.)

The highway blows me away—and the mysterious swamp intrigues me. So Mule and I pull off and explore it a bit, though one can't get too far into it from where we start. But instead of staying on 10E, I decide to pick my way down and see if I can find some of the poor communities we visited on that Greenpeace venture.

After prowling through a number of back roads and having no success in finding the places I was looking for, we head east to try to find the interstate again. Tooling along through some very pretty country, Mule and I eventually find ourselves behind a pickup truck pulling a trailer with a motorcycle strapped to it. As I'm in no hurry and enjoying looking over the motorcycle, we amble along easily and follow him around some sweeping curves, through some trees and up a rise, then slow at the top as he has to stop just ahead and below us for a red light. It appears that we've come to a significant highway, so the adventure is behind us. Or so I think.

"Uh oh," grunts Mule.

"What?"

"Look."

"Where?"

"Down."

I do. The rise we've stopped on is whatever you call that hump of land they sometimes build up for a train track. And we're at the top of it, so we're sitting astride a train track.

"Whoa."

"Yup."

The truck with the motorcycle is still ahead of us, waiting for the light to change. I look in the rearview mirror and there's a pickup truck right behind us, as well.

"Good thing there's not a train coming."

"You sure?"

I look both ways. "Don't see anything."

"Look again."

I do. "I don't . . . Oh shit."

"I'd say so."

It's hard to believe. There's a beam that looks a lot like a headlight on a train just coming around a curve a ways up the track.

"Holy shit!"

"Yup."

What the fuck? I can't go forward, so I put Mule in reverse and begin to back up, but the guy behind me doesn't seem to get it. I back up a bit and he moves a bit, but we're still on the goddamned tracks. Move, damnit! He moves a bit more, so I move a bit more, but the frigging train is actually coming down the track, right at us! Finally, he moves a bit more and we move a bit more, so we're finally off one set of tracks, but we're still straddling another set of tracks and I'm not sure which set of tracks the damn train is on. And now I hear him blaring his horn!

Mule grunts, "I don't like this."

I wave at the guy behind me, who moves a bit more and I back up as much as I can and just manage to get the front wheels over the second set of tracks without ramming into the asshole, when down comes the arm of the train guard that blocks the road across the tracks ahead of us—and in a split second I realize that there must be another one coming down right on top of us. I hit the gas again just as WHAM! the thing smacks Mule on top of the head and bounces off and down, just missing the hood as we push the guy behind us farther back! And the frigging train roars by as we both sit there shaking.

"What the fuck!"

Mule doesn't have much more to say. Nor do I. I don't even much like to think about what might have happened. As I explain to Mule later, "I could have gotten out, stepped away and watched, you know."

"Asshole," he mutters.

On the unusually quiet drive down to New Orleans I stop and buy something to clean and soothe the bump on his head.

DAY ELEVEN

Tuesday, May 20, 2008

CITY: NEW ORLEANS, LA
VENUE: OCTAVIA BOOKS

SPECIAL GUEST
Sister Helen Prejean

A bizarre day. More subjects than I can deal with in one day without falling into utter incoherence—as if I haven't already—are on tap. First thing in the morning I'm live on the air with KPFK radio in Los Angeles, discussing the Israeli/Palestinian issue on Margaret Prescod's *Sojourner Truth* show. One of the other guests is a Palestinian man who was, with his family, driven from his home by the Israelis in 1948. Now living in London, he's understandably angry about the lack of resolution of the Palestinian claims for the right of return or compensation. The other guest is an American Jewish woman who represents an organization, the name of which I can't remember, that opposes the ongoing Israeli occupation of the West Bank and its military actions against Gaza. I'm asked about my reasons for supporting President Jimmy Carter's recent visit to the region, and also about my own trips there and, in particular, about the events I was involved in related to an attempt by the then-leader of the U.S. branch of

Save the Children to suppress a report critical of Israel Defense Forces' treatment of Palestinian kids and, when that didn't succeed, to distance Save the Children U.S. from being associated with the report.

Needless to say, the Israeli/Palestinian issue is much too large, too complex and too volatile to be thoroughly discussed in an hour-long radio show, but it's important that some of these questions be addressed.

That behind me, Mule (who shows no sign of damage—or resentment—from being hit on the head yesterday) and I drive out to the University of New Orleans, in the north-central part of the city, for a live NPR interview with a Baltimore affiliate, which focuses on my appearance at the Enoch Pratt Free Library there next Sunday. It is a delightful hour with a very bright host and a lot of good callers.

Then, getting directions and some advice from the woman at WWNO (the local NPR affiliate) who hooked me up with Baltimore and monitored the call, we go to see some of the damage done by Hurricane Katrina near the university. This kind young woman, who works here every day, says she couldn't drive to work through this area for weeks after the storm without breaking into tears. Seeing it even now, so long after the events, one can understand the reaction. Vacant lots appear where houses once stood, many of the structures that remain are badly damaged and boarded up, some visibly moved from their foundations, while others have been cleaned up enough that people are able to live in them. It's very sobering. Work crews are here, still trying to repair the damage, steering traffic around the project at hand, and it's obvious that much remains to be done. This is—or at least was—a nice, middle-class neighborhood.

Next we head down to the Lower Ninth Ward, about which we've all heard so much. This is the area that was essentially submerged as a result of several breaks in levees and a very badly designed flow channel, resulting in the devastation that provided news footage and stories for months.

Getting down to the Lower Ninth is surprisingly easy, but at the same time very hard. It's crowded, the streets are narrow, the traffic is heavy and the level of poverty here is deeply depressing. Add to this the fact that the damage to the homes starts long before you come to what is technically the Lower Ninth Ward.

Mule and I note, in nearing the area, that we cross Desire, with nary a streetcar in sight.

The street I was urged to take is closed, so we maneuver our way further south, across a bridge over the now (hopefully) repaired levee, and into ground zero. It's as though a war was fought here. The homes are—or were—mostly woodframe, but there is a smattering of brick ones as well. And there is plenty of empty ground where no houses exist anymore. There are piles of wooden scraps that people once lived in and hung pictures on and slept beneath. Even the brick houses are mostly empty, boarded up, some of them obviously knocked off their intended footing. And even here, in this no-man's-land, some of the houses are occupied, with people sitting on the front porch talking, as though everything is normal.

The devastation continues, apparently for miles. Though I can't find the project that Brad Pitt has done so much for, it's clear that his type of energy has been emulated and amplified by the efforts of many good people from all over the country—and those who stayed on here—to make things right.

The devastation brings to mind a tour I was given of the post-Katrina damage to the Gulf Coast east of here in Mississippi and Alabama a few months after the storm. Seeing a four-story casino as long as a football field that had once been firmly situated just offshore now resting 100 yards inland atop what were once a group of houses, gives sphincter-tightening evidence of the true power of wind and water.

We drive east as far as St. Bernard Parish, stunned at the size and scope of the damage. Large shopping malls are ruined, boarded up, gone. The fact that the city has had the courage and the fortitude to come back to the degree it has is astounding. The fact that the Bush administration has been such a sorrowful failure in dealing with it appropriately is infuriating.

Chastened, we head back to the safety of the hotel.

At the appointed hour in the evening we make our way to Octavia Books on the western side of town, another in a line of good independent bookstores I've been fortunate enough to appear at on this trip. A sizable crowd for a small store, probably fifty or sixty people, listens to my story and asks really smart questions before I'm invited to sign a bunch of books. This group, I find, is peppered with some surprises. The Reverend Joe Doss, founder of Death Penalty Focus, the organization I've chaired for the past ten years, is here with his son Andrew. Joe, a retired Episcopal priest, now lives in New Orleans and it's a wonderful treat to see him. Also here is Sister Maureen Fenellan, who works with Sister Helen Prejean, the author of *Dead Man Walking*, the book, then movie, then opera, now play, that has done so much to move forward the dialogue on ending the death penalty. Sister Helen, herself probably the single most powerful voice for abolition in this country, caught a late plane from a speaking engagement in New York and can't introduce me, as had been hoped, but she will meet us at dinner. An Australian émigré named Rose, whose last name I missed, is here. She also works with

Sister Helen. And two other people who surprised me by showing up are dear friends and juggernauts for abolition: Scharlette Holdman, a legendary investigator and mitigation specialist; and Denny LeBoeuf, a gorgeous, powerful, indefatigable criminal defense lawyer whose laser-sharp mind and indomitable will provide nightmares for prosecutors.

Two people who approach me are transplanted Texans, now living in this city. They're here because he's an engineer, brought in to help with the reconstruction. They're staying beyond the agreed time because they have become emotionally involved in the struggle to rebuild this city. Very quiet, calm, shy, they are the kinds of people whose generous hearts make me know that we'll succeed in making this country live up to its promise.

Once done with my responsibilities at the bookstore, I follow Rose to a restaurant where Sister Helen, Deni, Maureen, Rose, a woman named Lily and another investigator, "Idaho Joe," and I enjoy a great dinner and wonderful conversation until I'm stuffed and almost asleep.

A full day.

DAY TWELVE

Wednesday, May 21, 2008

CITY OF ORIGIN: NEW ORLEANS, LA

MILES TRAVELED: 477

CITY OF DESTINATION: DECATUR, GA

VENUE: GEORGIA CENTER FOR THE BOOK/
DECATUR ARTS FESTIVAL

EVENT COSPONSOR

Southern Center for Human Rights

Heading out of New Orleans, we have plenty of time to get to Atlanta and a lot to think about. Mule is quiet, which is understandable, given what we saw yesterday. I am too. Heading out on 10E, we see more: the damage extends as far north as this highway, and it soon becomes clear from the hulks remaining that the flooding crossed the highway and destroyed homes and businesses even farther north.

It's hard to shake these images. We've all seen the pictures and heard the stories, but when you're in the midst of it, it's just so much more than you had thought. All these lives and dreams and hopes . . . just gone. I guess it's especially poignant when you're able to spend a comfortable night in a great bed—or a garage, in Mule's case—right down the street from all this horror.

The doorman at the hotel told me that his mother, whose house was completely destroyed, has just gotten the insurance settlement that will allow her to rebuild. Just now, almost three years after the storm. And how about all those whom the insurance companies are screwing with, those in the FEMA camps, living in poisonous trailers, those left without anything? He was philosophical about the fact that the heart of the city, the commercial district, was the initial focus of concern because of the need to bring back revenue, but all those other people . . .

Thinking of the trailers, I remember reading that some of the FEMA camps are located in the very Cancer Alley we toured those years ago. Talk about insult to injury.

The engineer from Texas at the bookstore last night said he was here to do an assessment right after the hurricane hit. He explained that television simply couldn't convey the reality of it—the stench of death, of rotting corpses, leaking gas, rotting food. He said they were finding body parts in the wreckage of the houses. It was impossible, he told me, to leave. He had to make the commitment to stay and help.

A bitter irony, when thinking about the failure of the Bush administration to organize a Marshall Plan–type response to this catastrophe, is remembering W.'s instantly "compassionate" response to the destruction of Trent Lott's Gulf Coast home. Help your friends . . .

And, let's not forget, "Heck of a job, Brownie!"

CRACK!

"Ouch!"

Mule takes a rock in the windshield. Made a hell of a noise, must have hurt. No actual crack or pit, but it hit hard. Then there are more, not as loud, but hitting other parts of the front end. It's a big truck ahead of us in the left lane, evidently carrying a load of rocks and losing some of them, so we pull over as far to the right as possible and speed past him before he buries us.

After a while, we come to an area where a series of coastline bridges are being rebuilt. What looks like a dozen huge cranes stab the sky. The work is necessary, obviously, but what a pain! On the westbound side, they're down to one lane and there's a line of cars backed up for half a mile. Sure hope that doesn't happen on this side. There's a reception at the library in Decatur, outside Atlanta, that starts at 5:30.

Crossing into Mississippi I note that the highway is new. Must have been badly damaged. I was here a few months after the hurricane and the destruction was incredible. Pass Christian, which we race by without time to go through now, was reportedly completely trashed. In Gulfport, which I did pass through before, a two-story house shows a watermark halfway up its second story to give passersby an idea of the height of the surge.

Thoughts of the dinner last night come to me. What an incredible group around Sister Helen! Their simple humanity is inspiring. Such good people doing such important work. They talked about two cases

SOUTHERN CENTER FOR HUMAN RIGHTS

The Southern Center for Human Rights (SCHR) is a nonprofit public interest law firm based in Atlanta, Georgia. Founded in 1976, SCHR's mission is to end capital punishment, mass incarceration, and other criminal justice practices that are used to control the lives of poor people, people of color, and other marginalized groups in the southern United States, and to build the power of those communities to transform the criminal justice system.

In the last thirty years, the Southern Center for Human Rights has:

- REPRESENTED HUNDREDS OF PEOPLE ON DEATH ROW ACROSS THE SOUTH, delaying and derailing sentences of death and exposing the both arbitrary and discriminatory nature of capital punishment. Our work has resulted in countless people being freed from the threat of state execution, and two unanimous United States Supreme Court decisions impacting the administration of the death penalty.

- FORCED COUNTY, STATE, AND FEDERAL GOVERNMENTS TO MAKE SIGNIFICANT IMPROVEMENTS IN PRISONS AND JAILS ACROSS THE SOUTH—to reduce overcrowding, provide adequate medical and mental health care, and to limit violence and abuse. Some of our largest wins have resulted in: an overhaul of South Carolina's entire prison

that stay with me: one having to do with a young woman condemned for the murder of a baby she was caring for. They're sure it was an accident and have dug up facts unknown to the defense at the time of trial that have stopped the execution and moved the court to order a new hearing. The other case, I presume a death case but don't know anything about it except for their description of the condemned woman: she'd had three abortions when a young girl, abortions to end pregnancies caused by her father.

God . . .

We move into Alabama, which is amazingly green, with trees as far as you can see. We're headed toward Montgomery where my friend Brian Stevenson runs the Equal Justice Initiative, but we don't have time to stop. In fact, I now realize, we don't have time for anything. I've spaced on the issue that Atlanta is in a different time zone. We lose an hour on this trip, so it's going to be damned near impossible to get to the reception on time—and the reception is for me.

system; major renovations in Louisiana's Angola Prison death row; shutting down Alabama's Morgan County jail; and improved HIV care in Limestone Prison in Alabama, resulting in an eighty percent drop in AIDS deaths.

- **Secured a statewide public defender system in Georgia.** SCHR's five-year campaign included six lawsuits, two reports, family organizing, and work with legislators and advocates to push for reforms of Georgia's indigent defense system. Georgia replaced a broken system of 159 different county-funded indigent defense systems with a comprehensive, statewide public defender system in 2005.
- **Put an end to illegal and inhumane criminal justice practices.** Through litigation, organizing, and media advocacy, SCHR has challenged the exploitation of the poor in the criminal justice system, and draconian and ineffective laws targeting pariah groups. In Clinch County, Georgia, the sheriff no longer charges people—including those who are found not guilty or whose charges are dismissed—a room-and-board fee for being incarcerated in the county jail. In 2006, we stopped the forced banishment of over 12,000 people from the state, when a misguided residency restriction law made it illegal for people on the sex offender registry to live in the state (while doing nothing to make our communities safer).

Shit! I press Mule as much as I dare; it wouldn't be a good idea to get stopped for speeding.

Roadwork, traffic, everything you can imagine gets in the way. Finally, I pull into the city and follow the directions to the library, but make a wrong turn and have to stop at a gas station to ask for help. Damn, I'm going to be a half-hour late even if I go straight there, without checking into the hotel and changing into better clothes. So I compromise. Pulling over, I run to the back of the car, get out a clean shirt and change right there on the street. I'm sure I look like a homeless guy who lives in his car—which, in a way, I am—but at least I'll feel a little more presentable.

They're waiting for me. All, of course, are dressed to the nines as I walk in wearing scruffy jeans, a T-shirt and a jacket, but they're all as gracious as can be and act like they understand completely, bless them.

I'm introduced around and explain my tardiness—and Shelley's absence (they were all looking forward to meeting her)—and get the chance to answer a few questions. When I explain that I haven't had time to check into the hotel and would have liked to have changed, they all insist it isn't necessary, but after a bit I ask their indulgence to let me go over there now, since there are a few minutes to spare before I'm to speak to the crowd gathering in the auditorium, and everyone graciously agrees. So I race out, drive the few blocks to the hotel, check in, run upstairs, grab a few things from my bag, make a lightning change of clothing and manage to get back to the library one minute before I'm to go on.

And after all the craziness, it turns out to be a great evening. First, I'm honored beyond words to be introduced by Steve Bright, the Executive Director of the Southern Center for Human Rights and a personal hero of mine. Steve is one of the brightest, most articulate, most dedicated and most effective opponents of the death system in this country. A man who could be getting wealthy in any other field of law, he has dedicated himself to this work and has become, due to his talent and selfless dedication, one of the most admired men in the country.

After an introduction by Steve, how can I miss? The auditorium is filled with what must be about 200 people and the exchange is lively and fun. Afterward, they actually sell out of books and I have more time to chat and answer questions as I'm signing them. I'm thrilled to learn that one of the people in the audience is Dr. Dean Wilcox of Emory University. Dean was on one of the trips I took to the Middle East and, now that I think about it, he was the one who raised the question tonight about how to resolve the Israeli/Palestinian dilemma. He may be surprised to find that he's in the book. A terrific man.

Because of the time difference, I am able to get back to the hotel in time to catch most of the first game of the Lakers/Spurs match-up and cheer my team on to recover from a twenty-point deficit halfway through the third quarter and pull off a win!

What a day—and night.

DAY THIRTEEN

Thursday, May 22, 2008

CITY OF ORIGIN: DECATUR, GA

MILES TRAVELED: 203

CITY OF DESTINATION: ASHEVILLE, NC

VENUE: MALAPROP'S BOOKSTORE/CAFÉ

EVENT COSPONSORS

People of Faith Against the Death Penalty, Veterans for Peace Chapter 099, Buncombe Green Party

The day starts with a yelp from Mule. The dashboard is yelling a message at me—well, it's not yelling, but it feels that way because it's scaring me. *MAINTENANCE REQUIRED*, it says.

What the hell could that be? Could Mule be suffering a delayed reaction from that bang on the head? Unlikely. Is there a serious malfunction in the very confusing power train? Of course that could be it, and I'd not have the faintest idea what to do about it. I can't even understand the diagram on the damned dashboard. But I've got to go to a television interview this morning and she seems to be running all right. It's just unnerving having that sign yelling at me.

I've already checked out of the hotel, so we head for the TV station, following the directions carefully laid out for me by Johanna Ingalls from Akashic Books, my guardian angel. Have you ever tried to follow the directions printed out from Google Maps or MapQuest or whatever?

They're very clear, in that they tell you every turn and every distance down to the tenth of a mile, but they're confusing as hell because they also tell you EVERYTHING the signs say, particularly when you're on a highway or freeway. And when you're without a navigator—mine being at home healing a broken hip—you can get yourself killed trying to read them, understand them and follow them—particularly when you're going a thousand miles an hour.

And imagine trying to follow these directions in Atlanta, Georgia. It's not possible! This is one of the most confusing cities I've ever driven in, outside of Dublin, London, and Washington, DC. Like the first two, the streets keep changing their names as you're going down them. Unlike the first two, these streets loop and roll around curves and go up and down hills.

Anyway, as I'm driving I realize—from the fact that I'm squinting—that I've left my sunglasses back at the hotel. And I also realize that I'm in denial about dealing with *MAINTENANCE REQUIRED*. What do I do? I guess I have to call Hertz, but that will probably mean taking Mule in for some kind of inspection and repair and I DON'T HAVE TIME FOR THAT! I have to do this interview, then I want to stop and see Steve Bright's outfit, and I have to drive to Asheville, North Carolina—TODAY!

And besides, I'm afraid that if there's something wrong with Mule they'll take her away from me. And I can't stand the thought of that. Like the song says, I've become accustomed to her face.

So what to do? There's only one thing to do in this kind of situation. I call Johanna. As always, she's Johanna-on-the-spot, right there and ready to fix things. She'll call Hertz and call me back. Then, while I'm in the calling business, I phone the hotel and ask the guy to check my (former) room and see if my sunglasses are there. He'll call me back.

So I keep wending my way through the confusing streets of . . . well, it's actually Decatur, Georgia, but it seems to be part of greater Atlanta . . . toward the television station.

Johanna calls me back and gives me a number for Hertz roadside assistance. They need to talk to me directly, she says. Okay. Then the guy from the hotel calls back. He has my sunglasses in hand and will hold them for me. Great. All I have to do is figure out how to get back there. Oh, for some bread crumbs.

Hertz roadside assistance asks if I have my rental agreement. I do. I give her the number. She goes away and comes back. What is the mileage on the car? she asks. I push the button (I've figured something out on the dashboard, I'm proud to say) to get away from *trip mileage* (which is now over 3,300) and find the total mileage on the car, which is 17,000 and something. She says, "No problem. The message means the car needs an oil change, but it's not actually necessary until you reach 19,548 miles, so when you get to that point you'll need to come into a local Hertz facility and we'll take care of it."

Whoa. Easy. What a relief. I'm not in danger of losing Mule.

(Let me clarify something here. As you may have noted, I sometimes refer to Mule as a "he" and sometimes as a "she." That's not an error. Mule is a hybrid, after all, and sometimes he seems to be a he and sometimes she seems to be a she. And I've become accustomed to both.)

Amazingly, I somehow arrive at West Peachtree Street, Northeast, and look for the TV station. (Peachtree Street, or streets, is a whole other story in Atlanta, but I don't have time for it here.) There's a gate on the right and a big TV station behind the fence, so I pull in, park and walk into the reception area. Two women behind the desk light up when they see me and give me the biggest, most charming welcome, talking about what fans they are. This is obviously the right place. I thank them and say I'm here to do *Atlanta & Company*.

"Oh, sorry," they say, "that's the other station, on down to the end of the street."

Pretty funny. So I thank them for the kind greeting and head back out.

At the right TV station I'm taken up to the studio and have a nice, live interview about the book and *M*A*S*H* and life and stuff. And then I'm done. Now we have to retrace the directions I've just followed to pick up my sunglasses. It's kind of like doing a puzzle, but after only a few screams and a couple of U-turns, we're there.

Glare compensated, we head downtown. Steve Bright's office is a great place right across from the Federal Court. Steve says that when they moved in, he's sure the Court said, "There goes the neighborhood." His crew of miracle workers, at least the ones I get to meet, are mostly women and mostly quite young, and the impact they're having is astounding. He says they've been able to fight the Georgia authorities to a virtual standoff. From twenty to thirty death convictions anually when he first set up shop in the '90s, they're down to just a couple per year, last year beating off all of them.

As a result, though they're still involved in a great deal of prison-condition lawsuits in Georgia, much of the death verdict appeal or trial defense they do out of this office is on Alabama cases, helping out Brian Stevenson and his Equal Justice Initiative.

Alabama, Steve says, is the pits. Brian is doing great work, but he's overwhelmed by the kill-'em-and-kill-'em-quick attitude over there. The judges are all elected in Alabama and they campaign on how tough they're going to be on crime and how much they support the death penalty. He says one of the things that stuns him is the absolute lack of any genuine feeling about it. Giving a death sentence is treated as casually as giving someone a traffic ticket. And worse, he says, the law provides a

judicial override, so a jury can convict someone and recommend life without parole but then the judges can—and sometimes do—override their recommendation and sentence the person (usually black) to death.

Georgia is killing someone tonight, so Steve clearly doesn't win them all here, but he says Alabama is becoming the next Texas.

This is a great guy, Steve Bright. He and Brian Stevenson and their staffs are truly American heroes, doing the toughest, most heartbreaking work by forcing the system to deal with real, caring, dedicated professionals and, when given a fair shot, beating the pants off them.

Asheville, North Carolina is supposed to be a three and a half

PEOPLE OF FAITH AGAINST THE DEATH PENALTY

The questions surrounding the death penalty are questions of the soul as well as of public policy. They are questions that demand discussion, debate, discernment, and resolution—or they will be left unexamined and unresolved in our congregations as much as in our legislatures and courtrooms. As such, political leaders will continue to resort to using the death penalty as a simple and false solution to violent crime.

People of Faith Against the Death Penalty is a resource and catalyst for exploring the questions and answers around the death penalty and violent crime. PFADP works to educate and mobilize faith communities to act to abolish the death penalty in the United States. Founded in 1994, PFADP is the only grassroots, faith-based national death penalty abolition group headquartered in the former Confederacy, where eighty percent of executions take place. PFADP encourages pastoral leaders and laypeople to reflect on our nation's use of capital punishment and to take personal responsibility to act for its abolition. PFADP has mobilized thousands of people and congregations to

hour drive and I have a radio interview at 6 p.m., so I say my goodbyes and soon we're flying along through northeast Georgia on Highway 85. The speed limit says seventy, but most of these folks are doing eighty or more, and Mule is keeping right up with them. Suddenly, just over the top of a rise, everything is stopped, or stopping, before us! The car ahead of me slams on its brakes and I slam on mine, he goes right and I go left, he barely misses a car in the lane to our right and Mule and I squirrel around a bit on the edge of the grassy median to our left, my eyes flashing from the mess in front of me to the rearview mirror to see if we're going to be hit from behind. No one smashes into anyone that I can see, but an SUV flashes by on my left and spins around out in the middle of the overgrown median, plowing up grass as he comes to a stop and sits there, obviously quite shaken.

The line of cars and trucks stretch out before us as far as I can see. And it's not a pretty sight. There's no exit and nothing to do, so we sit. The guy in the median sits as well. I look over at him as we have a chance to creep forward a bit and he looks to be okay, just allowing

reflect and take action toward abolishing the death penalty.

PFADP was founded explicitly on a vision of restorative justice, on working toward healing all affected by violence—victims, the community, and offenders—and we offer policy alternatives to the death penalty and retributive justice.

As an interfaith organization, PFADP is composed of Christians, Jews, Muslims, Buddhists, and people from other faith traditions (and some from no faith traditions). The religious leadership in America has now turned its thumb down on the death penalty. We believe that the Christian church must strengthen its role in undoing the harm it has caused through more than a millennium of giving its blessings and encouragement to this practice.

The work of PFADP's thousands of members across the United States has helped change the aesthetics of the politics of the death penalty. With PFADP's leadership, abolitionists are slowly gaining more control of the agendas around the issue, and they are nourishing a culture of abolition throughout America today that has begun to percolate into our courts and into our legislatures despite the fear and resistance of the leaderships of both dominant political parties. These changes will continue to grow if you get involved and make them grow.

the adrenaline to stop pumping.

I think of that jam-up I noted on the other side of the highway down in Louisiana yesterday. This is worse. Worse because we're in it, of course, but also worse because I can see for a hell of a distance and it's a parking lot.

So we sit awhile, then creep awhile, then sit awhile longer, then creep some more. It's awful. Every time we creep our way to a rise or around a corner, I pray the end will be suddenly visible. But no. A half-hour of this. Then another.

What to do? I call Johanna at Akashic Books, of course, and tell her the situation. I had thought we had plenty of time to get there for the radio interview, but if this keeps up, I don't know. She says she'll call and alert the guy I'm to meet that there may be a problem. And we creep. And sit. And creep.

Finally, after about an hour and a half of this crazy-making situation, during which I note that the creeping is wearing Mule's battery down to a very scary level, a sign tells me that we're nearing a town: Commerce, Georgia. Edging into the right lane, I see that there's enough paved surface beyond the legal right lane to slip along past the cars and trucks in front of us, so we move over and scoot along (pissing a lot of people off, I'm sure) until we come to the exit for Commerce and pull into the nearest gas station. Sure enough, I'm told, there is a way around the problem that brings you back to the highway above the accident, which is another mile or so up the road for the creepers. So off we race through the countryside and a couple of miles north find our way back to a Highway 85 that's clear as a bell.

But we're not going to make the interview. Johanna stays in touch and says the guy, Ronald, is being a prince. Not to worry, he says, if I make it on time, fine, and if not, we'll figure something else out. He's a fan, Johanna says, and it's his birthday, so he's hoping we can at least meet.

Racing through the beautiful, rolling, tree-covered hills of South Carolina, then passing into virtually the same landscape in North Carolina, makes me think of my friend John Denver's song about West Virginia. Wonderful song. Terrific man. What a talent. What a loss.

Once in Asheville I pull up and run into the hotel. Ronald is there with a friend and they tell me not to rush, take it easy, do what I need to do and they'll walk me over to Malaprop's, the bookstore. Nice folks.

At Malaprop's, there's a large crowd waiting. The event is cosponsored by People of Faith Against the Death Penalty (chaired by Steve Dear, whose brother John is the priest I met in Santa Fe), Veterans for Peace Chapter 099 (of which Ronald is a member), and the Buncombe Green Party. It's another warm and fun evening. Good questions are asked and a lot of stories are told. I love the mix of talking about the death penalty, the political situation, *M*A*S*H,* human rights, Shelley and whatever else is on people's minds. One woman asks about my association with the Cult Awareness Network and what I think about this terrible situation with the kids from the polygamous Mormon cult in Texas. A really tough one. I understand that there's been a ruling holding that the kids were not molested, something I personally find hard to believe.

One very touching thing happened tonight. When we were talking about the death penalty I mentioned the number of people exonerated from death row. I said this direct evidence of human error ought to be enough to end the use of state killing all by itself. I mentioned Glen Edward Chapman, the 127th death row exoneree who was freed last month here in North Carolina and is, as I understand it, living in Asheville.

Someone called out, "He's here."

I said, "Yes, here in Asheville."

She replied, "No, he's here," and pointed to a black man a couple of rows behind her.

I was knocked out that he was there. Fourteen years of this young man's life had been wasted as he was locked away by society for something he didn't do. Not only had he spent those years in prison, but under the torturous conditions of death row, knowing that you were lower than dirt, worthy only of being disposed of by a society that had determined you were not fit to live among them—or even to live. Fourteen years of humiliation and degradation by guards and an administration only concerned with its own preservation. Fourteen years of dehumanization by a system that offered you nothing but the promise of impending death.

I had read of Chapman's decision to get a job and show that he could be a productive citizen rather than becoming lost in anger and a desire to strike back because of the wrong that had been done him. I asked him to stand and told him there was, in my view, no way to repay the debt this society owed him. The audience gave him a warm welcome. If only the politicians who support this awful system had his courage . . .

After some books were signed and some pictures were taken—and I had a chance to talk further with Ed Chapman—I went to dinner at a vegan restaurant with Ronald, the birthday boy, and two of his Veterans for Peace colleagues.

And when I get back to my hotel room I learn that Steve Bright and those with whom he works have not lost after all. Samuel David Crowe was not executed. Two hours before he was to die, the Georgia State Board of Pardons and Paroles decided to commute his sentence to life in prison without parole, this after the 11th Circuit Court of Appeals had refused to consider a request for a stay because it had not been properly filed.

Two hours before they strap you down. How's that for torture?

DAY FOURTEEN

Friday, May 23, 2008

CITY OF ORIGIN: ASHEVILLE, NC

MILES TRAVELED: 246

CITY OF DESTINATION: RALEIGH, NC

VENUE: QUAIL RIDGE BOOKS & MUSIC

EVENT COSPONSORS

People of Faith Against the Death Penalty, North Carolina Justice Center

Asheville seems to be a bit of a hippie enclave in the North Carolina mountains, complete with shops, health food stores—not only natural food but vegan restaurants (like last night's)—and a lot of people looking like they're living in the '60s. I love it!

I picked up the *New York Times* at Malaprop's and the proprietor, a Hungarian refugee, said lovely things about last night and promised that the people here will work hard on all the issues we talked about.

Heading out 40E toward Raleigh, I'm struck by the vivid patches of wildflowers lining the entrances and exits from the highway. Fabulous colors; Shelley would have loved this.

This area is as green as Alabama, but the mountains give it a special grace. It's interesting that these mountains are the highest east of the Mississippi—Mount Mitchell, the highest of all, is less than 7,000 feet. Not so tall when compared to the Rockies, but they sure are beautiful.

The drive to Raleigh is long and largely uneventful. I'd been warned by last night's dinner companions that the North Carolina cops are very vigilant about speeders. "They'll give you five miles over the posted limit," I was told, "but any more than that, they'll be all over you." And as we tooled along, that understanding seemed to be widely shared. With few exceptions, people pretty much stayed to about five miles over the limit, so Mule and I went along fine for most of the way. Then I saw a backup on the other side, heading west. *Sure glad we're not going that way*, I thought. Then, remembering the one I'd seen in Louisiana and what happened after that, I hoped it wasn't an omen. But sure enough, as we neared the turnoff for Raleigh, red lights appeared ahead of us and pretty soon we were at a dead stop.

Traffic is the bane of modern civilization, American style. Too many people in the cities. Fortunately, though, we were able to cut over, take a turnoff and avoid what looked like a continuing snarl up ahead.

NORTH CAROLINA JUSTICE CENTER

The North Carolina Justice Center is the state's leading progressive advocacy and research organization. Our mission is to eliminate poverty in North Carolina by ensuring that every household has the services, resources, and fair treatment it needs to access opportunities to achieve economic security. To that end, we do advocacy and research in the areas of public education, health care, the state budget, taxes, consumer protections, and housing.

We are unique in that we employ five strategies in our work for progressive change:

- Lobbying to secure laws and policies that improve the lives of low- and moderate-income families
- Litigation of high-impact cases that protect and expand the rights of disadvantaged groups
- Research on how policies impact low-income North Carolinians and how they can be improved
- Community education that improves local groups and individuals
- Media outreach that shapes public opinion

The Justice Center includes a nine-member legal team that stands up for the rights of immigrants and migrant workers—an especially urgent need in our state. Law-enforcement agencies in seven North Carolina counties have signed up to partner

Checking into the hotel, I have time to see how far behind I am on my e-mail, but can't do much about it as we have to get over to Quail Ridge Books & Music for tonight's event. Steve Dear's organization here in North Carolina, People of Faith Against the Death Penalty, is cosponsoring again this evening, as is the North Carolina Justice Center, which is run by a very bright woman named Jill Diaz. Introduced by Nancy Olson, the proprietor, Jill opens the evening with an explanation of the work of her organization, then throws it to Steve, who introduces me.

Like his brother John, the activist priest, Steve is a sweet and deeply dedicated man who has done wonders to raise the level of understanding about the horrors of the death penalty for the people of North Carolina. They've come close to getting a moratorium here and I expect to see more exciting developments in the future. North Carolina has had eight men exon-

with federal immigration enforcement, which they believe gives them license to harass immigrants and engage in racial profiling. This leaves Latino communities without law enforcement they can trust to protect them.

The Justice Center is leading an effort to ensure police and sheriffs' departments grant immigrants the human and legal rights they are due. We monitor the conditions in detention areas, help families locate loved ones who have been arrested, and guide immigrant communities in making preparations should they become the targets of a raid. We also spread the word about the aggressive, discriminatory, and sometimes unconstitutional immigrant enforcement tactics that are being used.

The Justice Center helps hundreds of low-income immigrants every year apply for legal status, including asylum. The burdens of proof for asylum seekers are almost insurmountable, and the legal requirements are impossible for anyone without experience in immigration law to negotiate. That's where the Justice Center steps in, providing free legal services to those whose lives depend on having a competent attorney but who cannot afford to hire one.

The Justice Center is committed to supporting opportunity and prosperity for everyone in North Carolina, regardless of race, ethnicity, or country of origin.

erated from their death rows, two within the past few months—Glen Edward "Ed" Chapman, who I met in Asheville, was freed in April and

Levon "Bo" Jones was just released on the second of this month. Steve and PFADP will not let this go unnoticed.

The crowd here at Quail Ridge is huge, filling the area set aside for seating and spilling into the aisles of the store and up around the counters behind. And once again, it's a hoot! People are thoughtful and attentive, open to the ideas I offer and full of questions, comments, concerns and, of course, a palpable love and appreciation for *M*A*S*H*.

Perhaps one should expect such a warm and wonderful embrace from a group of people willing to come to an event sponsored by organizations such as Steve's and Jill's, but for me there's always that old actors' fear of coming out and having to play to an empty house. That has certainly not been the case on this trip, I must say, but the insecurity remains, nonetheless.

In any event, it's a wonderful evening and a great discussion. Afterward, between signing books and having pictures taken, I'm able to meet three people from Nazareth House Catholic Worker, with whom I've had some communication. Though I didn't get here early enough to visit their place, as I had hoped, they have come to hear me and say hello. The Catholic Worker movement grew out of the life and teachings of Dorothy Day, and involves a commitment to nonviolence, voluntary poverty, prayer, and providing hospitality for the homeless, exiled, hungry, and forsaken. Catholic Workers protest injustice, war, racism, and violence of all forms, but this community, run by Scott Langley, an Amnesty International Death Penalty Abolition Coordinator, focuses on providing refuge and support for family members visiting loved ones on death row.

Heroes abound in this world.

After conversation is had, books are signed, pictures are taken (including a sweet interlude with Abbi, a six-year-old whose family has endured a three-hour drive to bring her here to meet "BJ," her favorite *M*A*S*H* character) and people are gone, Steve Dear and I take four young friends of his out to dinner. Speaking of heroes, these lovely young women, all in their early twenties and all college graduates, are Jesuit Volunteers. The Jesuit Volunteer Corps offers young women and men the opportunity to work full time for justice and peace. Living in community and existing on the smallest of stipends from the organization—this augmented by another small contribution from the group to which they're assigned—the JVs give a year of their lives to work with a social justice organization.

The dinner is lively and full of laughter, the young women bright and attractive and fun. One of them, Amanda, works with Steve at People of Faith Against the Death Penalty. Alex works with an organization dealing with victims of AIDS, Chelsea with a group providing shelter and support for the homeless, and Melissa an organization offering support for immigrants, especially, as I understand it, focusing on issues of domestic violence.

Charming, vibrant young women giving their time, talents and a good measure of their hearts to people in need. Damned impressive, I think, and evidence that this country really does have the capacity to live up to its promise.

After all that, I still get back to the hotel in time to catch the last few minutes of the Lakers/Spurs game—a romp for the Lakers, who are up 2–0 in a best-of-seven series!

DAY FIFTEEN

Saturday, May 24, 2008

CITY OF ORIGIN: RALEIGH, NC

MILES TRAVELED: 276

CITY OF DESTINATION: WASHINGTON, DC

VENUE: BUSBOYS AND POETS

EVENT COSPONSORS

Service Employees International Union, Public Citizen, Greenpeace

U p early, grab a quick shower and hustle down to wake up Mule. It's raining this morning, a surprise after the beautiful weather we've been enjoying. But hearing from Shelley last night about the tornadoes (tornadoes!) in Southern California, I guess I don't have much to complain about. The drive to DC is supposed to take four and a half hours, per my itinerary, and I have a TV interview in the afternoon; the book event is an early one, from 4 to 5:30 p.m. It's Saturday and I guess it's the Memorial Day weekend (the downside of a trip like this is that you get so focused you lose touch with what's happening in the world), so the early schedule is an attempt to compensate for that.

The radio tells me that something like thirty million cars will be on the road this weekend. It feels like they're all on mine. And you know the problems I was talking about in Atlanta with the directions printed out by computer? Well, they're frustrating and confusing enough when you're by yourself and trying to read and understand and turn and go 0.2 miles and stop and do a U-turn and then go again and somehow manage to not get killed, but it's even worse when they're WRONG. I knew it, I knew it, I knew it! Even Mule knew it. The damned directions sent me west when I knew they should send me east, but they were so confusing that I doubted myself and followed them, only to end up screaming bloody murder as I went around a cloverleaf twice trying to get back in the other direction with every North Carolinian who was up too early on Saturday morning honking and swearing at me. I probably broke more laws in that one maneuver than in my entire driving career.

But finally, calm again—I think Mule was actually scared that I had entirely lost it—and headed in the right direction, things smoothed out, the rain went away and we sailed up through Virginia.

Shelley called, which was early for her and it worried me a touch. It turned out that she was worried too. She was hearing strange noises coming from our bedroom fireplace and she was afraid some animal might have gotten trapped in the chimney. It had poured rain during the night, she said, and she wondered if it was possible that some creature had crawled into the top of the chimney to get away from the weather and gotten trapped.

My daughter Erin is there with her and she came in and thought she could hear something walking on the roof. As we talked over the possibilities, I tried to reassure her that it was unlikely that anything could have gotten into the chimney, but I really didn't know for sure. Shelley once had a bad scare when some raccoons tore shingles off the roof of another house and she was told by the animal welfare people that they sometimes actually work their way into the house.

That was clearly on her mind at this point, as it was on mine, but neither of us seemed to want to mention it. As she pointed out later, if some animal came down the chimney and she had to get out of the room in a hurry, that wouldn't be an easy thing to do, given her hip.

Fortunately, as it turned out, the problem was being created by huge blackbirds that were congregating on the chimney. Erin's investigation seems to have scared them off, so we were all able to calm down.

Now, racing along just north of Richmond, I see a worrisome thing. The southbound traffic across the median is stopped. "I don't like seeing that," I say to Mule. "Every damn time it happens over there it seems to happen on this side too, sooner or later."

Mule just snorts.

"Okay," I say, "but humor me. Keep your eyes peeled."

We were actually doing well. I figured at the rate we were going we'd be in DC by 1:30, I could check into the hotel, change, have plenty of time to do the TV interview and then casually stroll into Busboys and Poets, the bookstore/café on 14th Street, Northwest, in plenty of time, cool, unruffled, suave, debonair . . .

SERVICE EMPLOYEES INTERNATIONAL UNION

With two million members in the United States, Canada, and Puerto Rico, the Service Employees International Union (SEIU) is the fastest-growing union in the Americas.

SEIU's local union affiliates and state councils represent the people we see every day: nurses, doctors, home care providers, nursing home workers, janitors, security officers, child care providers, public employees, and workers in many other service professions. It is the most diverse union in America, with a leadership that reflects its ranks: more than half of our members are represented by local unions led by women or people of color.

Under the leadership of President Andy Stern and Secretary Treasurer Anna Burger, more than a million workers have united in SEIU since 1996. This has made SEIU the largest union of health care and property service workers and second-largest public employee union. As SEIU has grown, it has pioneered new models for workers to win a voice on the job. It has spearheaded bold new partnerships with community allies, employ-

. . . Oh crap! Brake lights! No way to exit, nothing to do but slow down, and down, and down. Pretty soon we're stopped. The cars on the right are still slipping by, so we ease over there and get a bit further along, but pretty soon everyone's stopped. "Did I tell you, Mule? Did I tell you?"

No snort this time.

Sirens, lights flashing. After sitting there for a long time, I step out to see if I can get a sense of what has happened. I don't know if there are other cars involved or not, but about a hundred yards ahead, a big semi has obviously lost control and it's a mess. The tractor part is upside down on the left side of the three-lane highway, actually up on the hillside, while the trailer is stretched out across two of the three lanes with its rear end hanging over a slope on the right side. Cops are converging from every direction, ambulances come down the perimeter of the road, a big wrecker rolls in, and we sit, unable to go forward or backward, with what are clearly hundreds of cars, maybe thousands, lining up behind us.

It is awful. Clearly, someone is hurt, possibly badly hurt, so one needs

ers, and other organizations to unite workers in the union.

SEIU is among the most powerful political forces in America. Fighting for issues like quality, affordable health care for all, wages that support families, a secure retirement, and freedom for workers to join a union, our members lobby for a proworker agenda on Capitol Hill, work to elect proworker candidates and to hold elected officials accountable.

During the 2008 presidential primary season, SEIU required all candidates seeking the union's endorsement to submit a detailed universal health care plan and to "Walk a Day in the Shoes" of an SEIU member by spending a day on the job with them. Six of the major presidential candidates accepted SEIU's challenge. SEIU endorsed Barack Obama for president in February 2008.

Through tireless organizing and tough political action, SEIU continues to be a driving force for change that affects working families. We are winning better wages, health care, and more secure jobs, while uniting our strength with our counterparts around the world to help ensure that workers, not just corporations and CEOs, benefit from today's global economy.

to keep priorities in order, but . . . you find yourself wondering . . . how long is this going to take?

Well, the answer is, a long time. We all sit there for about an hour and a half. I call the TV show and the producer tells me they'll wait. It is to be taped and shown tomorrow, so they're okay and willing to be patient. So we sit. People from cars lined up as far back as I can see have left their vehicles and walked down to the line where the fire people have stopped everybody.

Gives you a lot to think about, seeing something like that.

And there are practical considerations. Mule doesn't like to idle for long periods—or to creep, as I discovered the other day. His battery runs down.

Anyway, they finally get the injured taken away and eventually clear the roadway, so we ease into one lane and speed off toward DC. I call the producer and say it looks like I'll have to come straight there without checking into the hotel and changing, but I'll need them to be sure to get me out in time for the bookstore thing. She reassures me it is no problem.

PUBLIC CITIZEN

Public Citizen is a nonprofit public interest organization that represents consumers in the courts, executive branch agencies, and Congress. Based in Washington, DC, the national watchdog group has been fighting in the halls of power for the rights of ordinary citizens for more than thirty-five years. Corporations have lawyers, lobbyists, and experts in Washington; the public should as well.

Public Citizen's unassailable research exposes facts that people can use to hold government and corporations accountable. Public Citizen campaigns focus on safer drugs and motor vehicles, public health, access to the courts, government ethics and transparency, fair trade policies, and sustainable energy. The organization ensures that people have access to government information so they can be active citizens.

This is the group that secured airline passengers' rights when they are bumped from flights, won the release of Nixon's secret White House tapes, fought for twenty years to get lifesaving air bags in cars, successfully petitioned to have the dangerous herbal supplement ephedra removed from the market, secured strong ethics laws for federal lawmakers and

The show is something called *Out of the Box,* and has a larger audience outside the U.S. than in, much of it throughout the Middle East, so we get to talk a lot about the war in Iraq, about the Bush/Cheney policies, international relationships and the works. She has obviously read the book and asks me a bunch of questions about my trips to various parts of the world, allowing for an unusually frank political interview, not the tap dancing that passes for discourse in most of the media today.

lobbyists, blocked new coal plants in Texas, fought for stronger fuel economy standards, and much more.

Public Citizen exposes how much money various corporate interests raise for lawmakers, pressures Congress to repeal tax subsidies now given to wealthy oil companies, warns of the dangers of nuclear power, and successfully petitions to have dangerous prescription drugs removed from the market. Our lawyers argue—and more often than not, win—precedent-setting public interest cases before the U.S. Supreme Court, fifty-five cases to date. Public Citizen publishes a significant online health resource, www.WorstPills.org, which provides patients with an independent, second opinion about the safety and efficacy of prescription drugs.

In addition to lobbying for the people, testifying before Congress, and delivering timely news and reports to the media, Public Citizen builds strong coalitions with other nonprofit groups to more forcefully advance the consumer agenda.

Public Citizen is funded solely by memberships, foundation grants, and publication sales; it takes no corporate or government money, so it remains fiercely independent. Public Citizen works relentlessly, never giving up until reforms are won.

Racing off to Busboys and Poets, I get there just at 4 p.m. and there is quite a crowd waiting, which surprises me again. This event is cosponsored by the Service Employees International Union, Public Citizen and Greenpeace. Rick Hind, who handles government relations for Greenpeace, introduces me. A good guy, Rick has been in the struggle on the important issues for years and is a great friend and a wonderful resource.

One of the founders of Iraq Veterans Against the War is there, as is a woman from the Nuclear Information Resource Center. Tina Richards, the woman whose TV show I had just done, surprises me and shows up too. And a particular thrill is that my old friend Janet Shenk is here. Back in the days of the struggle against the Reagan administration's war in El Salvador, Janet was one of the true heroes, accompanying us on delegations, acting as a translator in meetings, arranging connections that no one else could make happen. The coauthor of *El Salvador: The Face of Revolution,* Janet is one of the brightest and most committed people in the movement for social justice today, whether in Latin America, the Middle East or here at home.

A representative from Congressman John Conyers's office is there too, wanting to recruit me into a single-payer health

> ### GREENPEACE
>
> Mike Farrell has been a great friend and ally of Greenpeace and the environmental movement for decades. Long before Hurricane Katrina, Mike joined Greenpeace in a 2001 "Celebrity Bus Tour" of Louisiana's Cancer Alley. The tour was organized by our legendary environmental justice leader Damu Smith and also included poet Alice Walker and Representative Maxine Waters (D-CA). They heard painful accounts of illnesses, deaths, and the routine denial of the petro-chemical industry responsible for the pollution. Mike wrote movingly about it on his website.
>
> After more than a decade of organizing, Damu was diagnosed with cancer in 2005 and tragically died a year later at fifty-four. Damu worked tirelessly to organize rainbow coalitions that defeated industry efforts to expand in low-income African American communities. One community's heroism against Shell Chemical was chronicled in a book by Steve Lerner, *Diamond: A Struggle for Environmental Justice in Louisiana's Chemical Corridor*. In addition to the pollution, workers and residents live in constant fear of another Bhopal disaster. Since 9/11, the vulnerability of chemical plants to terrorism has intensified these concerns. Greenpeace is asking Congress to require chemical plants to switch to safer chemicals and processes to eliminate these risks.

care campaign they're setting up. Conyers has been very helpful in a venture I'm currently involved with, trying to free the Angola 3, so it's possible we may soon be working together on something else.

It is another terrific event, with lots of good discussion about activism, the problems in the world, and whether there are reasons to hope. There are.

During the book signing, Gil and Susan introduce themselves. Though we'd never met personally, through a mutual friend they've been recipients of a torrent of e-mail articles and musings I send to a growing list. Gil is a former legislator and Susan had been—up until yesterday when Senator Clinton made a remark that Susan disagreed with—a committed Hillary Clinton supporter. No longer.

After people have cleared out, Rick, his fiancée Robin, Janet, her husband Steve (who works with the SEIU) and their beautiful daughter Olivia, fresh off the soccer field, and I stay on at Busboys and Poets for a fine dinner.

A long day and a good one.

Day Sixteen

Sunday, May 25, 2008

City of Origin: Washington, DC

Miles Traveled: 40

City of Destination: Baltimore, MD

Venue: Enoch Pratt Free Library

Event Cosponsors

American Friends Service Committee, ACLU of Maryland

A bit of confusion this morning. I was supposed to get a call for a phone interview, but it didn't come through. Fortunately, I went online just before leaving for Baltimore and got an e-mail from Johanna saying there is a problem with the hotel's phones. The reporter had tried to call but hadn't been able to get through. I have to leave, but give her my cell number and we connect as Mule and I are trying to find our way out of DC.

Have you ever tried driving in DC? I have a good sense of direction and I've driven in some pretty tough places, but DC is nuts. (Yes, for driving too.) Grids and spokes and one-way streets.

(A digression: I went online to get the name of the man who laid out the city—Pierre L'Enfante, if you care—so I could identify and cast aspersions on him as the madman who designed the layout of this nutty place. But I would have been doing it to have fun. And . . . well . . . the first entry on Google is all about how L'Enfante was a Freemason and, according to the whiz kid who wrote up this site, "The street design in Washington, DC, has been laid out in such a manner that certain Luciferic symbols are depicted by the streets, cul-de-sacs and rotaries."

Really! All I was going to do was make fun of the crazy quilt pattern of these streets and assert that no rational driver can be expected to find his or her way through this city without a guide dog, and suddenly I'm treated to an essay by someone who says, "You are about to learn that the U.S. Government is linked to Satanism." He (or she) says L'Enfante "hid certain occult magical symbols in the layout of U.S. Governmental Center. When these symbols are united they become one large Luciferic, or occultic, symbol."

The writer actually goes on at great length with this stuff, pointing out more symbols and making connections with Freemasonry and devil worship that are so bizarre it makes me want to laugh. I mean, sure, I think Dick Cheney is a scary, out-of-control, power-worshipping, war-mongering bastard, but I really don't buy that he's Satan.

Anyway, sorry for the digression, but the whacko stuff that people spend their time thinking up or buying into sometimes makes me wanna holler . . . No offense intended to any of you who share this view that "the American flag is the symbol of the Brotherhood and the Brotherhood is linked to Satanism.")

So where was I? Oh yeah. Mule and I are trying to read the damned directions to get out of this Luciferic city at the same time as I'm doing an interview with a young woman writing for something called *Critical Moment*. I guess I should have realized that someone writing for something with that name probably wasn't going to be asking me about my favorite *M*A*S*H* episode.

And she didn't. It was, in fact, a long and very serious interview about my views on political activism, social justice, whether there is a realistic possibility to change a system that doesn't respond to the needs of the people, whether it would be fair to label ours a system of "white supremacy," and other thought-provoking questions. It was an interesting and challenging interview that I would have loved to have done while sitting in a quiet place with time to think—and perhaps a drink. Instead, I was trying to pilot Mule through the Satanic rotaries and around the occultic corners of Washington, DC on a holiday weekend in order to get to a book gig in Baltimore. And again, the directions I was required to periodically take my eye off the road, at the risk of my life, to read and follow were, at a "critical moment," WRONG!!!

I don't want to make excuses here, of course, but if anyone ever reads an interview with me in something called *Critical Moment* and finds it to be disjointed, erratic, long-winded, semicoherent, periodically interrupted by bursts of cursing, hysterical laughter or, quite possibly, a fit of sobbing, be kind.

The interview concludes and finally, having found the right way to get on 295 North to Baltimore, it is as if a new day has dawned. Mule and I move along swimmingly, even though there are only three little squares on the gas meter. By the time we get to Baltimore there are just two, but I get so involved in figuring out which way we are supposed to turn that I space on filling the tank.

Parked, checked into the hotel and all is lovely. Once in the room I get a call from my friend Rick Schaeffer, a lawyer whom I had met as part of a delegation to the Middle East almost thirty years ago and who subsequently helped us in a campaign to save an innocent man—Joe Giarratano—from Virginia's electric chair. Rick is looking forward to the event at the Enoch Pratt Free Library and seeing me for dinner afterward, but had called the library to be told that it is closed today.

Hmmm. It is Sunday. And on top of that it is the Memorial Day weekend, or so I'm told. Maybe I'd better check. I call the woman in charge and leave a message asking if the event is still on and quickly get a call back assuring me that it is. However, she says, the library is normally closed on Sundays and, with the holiday, she isn't quite sure what to expect in terms of turnout. She has, she assures me, done a lot of promotion, but . . .

Ah well, I'm here. What the hell.

At the appointed time, Mule and I make our way to the library. Seeing again the two squares on the fuel gauge, I make a mental note to find a gas station but see none.

Outside the library, in one of the windows, there's a huge picture of little old me, with a big sign announcing the event today. Big damned picture! I wonder how they do that.

Inside, the event is to be held in the Edgar Allan Poe room. Evidently Ed was from Baltimore. When I get to the room—no visible ravens— there's a pretty nice crowd already inside, which is reassuring after the disclaimer, and as the appointed starting time approaches, more people continue to trickle in.

The woman who had organized it brings me in to meet the book dealer who is handling sales and the woman from the ACLU of Maryland who will introduce me, as they are cosponsoring the event.

A man sitting in the back row turns and says hello to me and I am stunned. It is Danny Porfirio. This guy had contacted me on the *M*A*S*H* set many years ago asking if I'd read something he had written. He passionately wanted to be a writer and had had no luck in getting anyone to look at his work. He reached out to me because we were both ex-Marines and the story he had written was about his time in the service, so he hoped, he said, that I'd at least take a look.

What are you gonna do? I wrote back and said I couldn't promise to get to it soon, but if he'd be patient I'd look at it and give him my opinion. He was so grateful it was embarrassing. I'm sure it was months before I got to this tome he had sent me, but I finally read it and wrote back to him, saying that I really didn't think it was a movie, but that he clearly had talent and I encouraged him to continue writing.

A few months later he sent me a short story about orphaned twin brothers, one of whom was a brilliant medical intern and the other was a slow boy who worked on a garbage truck. Though it took nine years to get it made, it became *Dominick and Eugene,* the first feature film my partner Marvin Minoff and I produced, starring Tom Hulce, Ray Liotta, and Jamie Lee Curtis.

Hell of a movie, if I do say so myself. Other than *M*A*S*H,* the project I'm most proud of. Do see it if you haven't.

By the time I'm introduced, the room is full, with standing room only. Must be close to a hundred people. Pretty nice, these Baltimoreans. And the afternoon turns into another great, warm, funny experience with us exchanging thoughts and views on all the issues I bring up and more. I'm knocked out by the hope and the excitement people express about what this country is capable of if we can only elect the proper leadership. One woman asked me what I thought were the three most critically important things we had to do to get this country back on track. I said, "Elect Barack Obama, elect Barack Obama, elect Barack Obama."

It got a great reaction.

After signing books and posing for pictures I get another chance to give Danny a hug—and promise to read some more things he's written.

Then Rick and I go out to dinner to catch up. He takes me to an Afghan restaurant owned by Hamid Karzai's brother. Unfortunately, he isn't there. I would have loved to ask him some questions.

Starting up Mule I hear a grunt. Uh oh.

"Yeah, I see we're down to one square."

Grunt.

"Yes, I know I said I'd never let it happen again."

"Liar!"

"Hey, easy. People make mistakes, you know?"

"Huh! People who get all stuck up about having their picture in the window."

"Whoa! Cheap shot."

Grunt.

"Look, Mule, I'm sorry. We'll find a station, I promise."

Grunt.

"Hang in there, pal."

Grunt.

By now I understand that "grunt" probably means "asshole." And I know if we get down to battery again, I'm toast.

You ever prowl the streets of Baltimore looking for a gas station? Don't. Finally, through the kindness of strangers, we stagger into a station in south Baltimore—and, thank God, they are open.

"See, pal? I wouldn't put you through that again."

Grunt.

That, and the Lakers lost to the Spurs tonight. You don't think Mule . . . ?
Nah.

DAY SEVENTEEN

Monday, May 26, 2008

CITY OF ORIGIN: BALTIMORE, MD

MILES TRAVELED: 192

CITY OF DESTINATION: NEW YORK, NY

VENUE: MADIBA RESTAURANT

EVENT COSPONSOR

Brooklyn for Peace

Got out of Baltimore with no problem. Mule is behaving nicely, thank you, so I may have been forgiven for the gas gaff—for being a fuel fool.

Speaking of Baltimore, did you know there is a Washington Monument here that predates the one in Satan's town? (I know, I know, but the detail in all that raving about DC was really weird . . . and who knows?) Anyway, yes, there is a very tall, cylindrical, and quite imposing structure in a square at Charles and Monument streets in the Mount Vernon Cultural District of Baltimore that was built twenty years before the monument we all know about in DC. And, I learned, Annapolis was the capital of our country for a short time, from late 1783 to mid 1784. Marylanders are very proud of their history. Well, except, maybe, for Spiro Agnew . . .

And one wonders at the statue of Chief Justice Roger Taney only a few steps away from the tribute to Washington. Expected to go down in history as one of the great chief justices of the Supreme Court, his place in the record books was forever tainted by his opinion in the 1857 Dred Scott case, in which he wrote of "that unfortunate race" which had "been regarded as beings of an inferior order, and altogether unfit to associate with the white race, either in social or political relations, and so far unfit that they had no rights which the white man was bound to respect."

There is some irony in the fact that Taney died on the very day Maryland abolished slavery.

It's a rich history we share, though not all of it inspires pride.

Driving north on the complex of roadways leading to New York takes us onto the New Jersey Turnpike. Speaking of abolition, I smile as we enter the state, thinking with satisfaction of New Jersey's courageous decision to abolish the death penalty in December of '07, an historic act that may move other states to do the same. I explain to Mule that Death Penalty Focus, the organization I chair, gave an award this past April to Governor Corzine and New Jerseyans for Alternatives to the Death Penalty (NJADP) for their courage.

Mule is unmoved.

"Hey, pal," I say, "the first state to abolish the death penalty in the modern era; it's a big step!"

"For people."

"Well, yeah. Yeah, I guess that's right. Hybrids don't kill their own, do they?"

Grunt.

"Right. Okay, people are odd. Present company excepted, of course?"

Silence.

"Huh. Well, we're working on it. Maybe Maryland will take the hint and be next."

Time for a bite. Don't tell anyone, especially the cops, but I'm getting pretty good at steering with my knees. I mean, you know, you don't want to pull over every time you have to peel a banana or take your vitamins. You'd never get anywhere. I've got this huge bag where I stash all my snacks and pills and herbs, and some things have to be unscrewed or ripped open or counted, and a guy needs two hands, you know?

Rush Limbaugh is at it today—I guess, like Sean, he's at it every day. What a windbag. He's terribly proud of this Operation Chaos nonsense. But I wonder, you know? I mean, except for a few true idiots, don't you think it's all bullshit? Here he is taking credit for wreaking all kinds of havoc in the "Democrat" race, causing Hillary to stay in and cut up Obama, and oh lordy, how he's looking forward to rioting in Denver during the "Democrat" convention.

Give it a rest, Rush.

Okay, we've suffered through the lines at the tollbooths (it's expensive to use these roads!), the incredible array of confusing signs, off-ramps, exits and construction, and now, finally into and through the Holland Tunnel, we're wending our way past more confusing signs, turns, exits and construction in Manhattan to get to the hotel.

In case you haven't been able to tell from this aimless soliloquy, today is a sort of day off. After checking in and changing, all we have to do is drive to Brooklyn and appear at a fundraiser for Brooklyn for Peace at a South African restaurant called Madiba.

I'm confused by the directions, of course, and get us lost in Chinatown, but Mule noses her way fearlessly to the Manhattan Bridge, across into Brooklyn, and even finds a parking place across from Madiba, where we connect with Johanna, Johnny, and Ibrahim from Akashic Books—and Cassie, Ibrahim's friend.

Brooklyn for Peace has made the book a premium for everyone who paid the tariff this evening, which is very nice, so I'm to say a few words. It's a great crowd, very lively, very enthusiastic, very open about their politics and forthright in their advocacy. It's a pleasure to hear their enthusiastic response to the guy running the show. He then presents a fellow who does a very funny riff as a CIA agent—à la Gary Trudeau's Duke—cleverly lampooning all the right-wing craziness. The food, served family style, is plentiful and very good. In the middle of it all I'm asked to say my few words—I clearly don't have to sell this crowd on anything, so I just cheer them on and take a few questions. Then it's time to have some dessert while signing a few books. One feisty older woman perfectly captures the night for me by saying, when I ask how she wants me to personalize her book, "Just make it out to *Dear Comrade*."

Rush, Sean, stay the hell out of Brooklyn!

DAY EIGHTEEN
Tuesday, May 27, 2008

CITY: NEW YORK, NY
VENUE: STRAND BOOKSTORE

EVENT COSPONSORS
Center for Constitutional Rights, The Nation Magazine

With two radio interviews scheduled today, I rouse Mule and we risk the hand-to-hand combat that constitutes driving in Manhattan. Johanna has found a Firestone dealer that has an arrangement with Hertz. So in order to get *MAINTENANCE REQUIRED* to stop yelling at me from the dashboard, I simply have to get Mule to this place, go on to my radio stuff and come back afterward and pick her up, all paid for by Hertz.

Or at least that's the way it's supposed to go.

The drive, through a lengthy tunnel and up the Westside Highway to Tenth Avenue and up from there to 26th Street, is surprisingly easy. The rest is more complicated.

The place is squeezed into the northwest corner of Tenth and 26th, surprisingly small and, shall we say, not the image of "the Firestone dealer" Mr. Firestone probably broadcasts on TV. The few feet of lot in front of the service bays is crammed with trucks, cars, trailers, and machinery. Leaving Mule illegally parked on the corner, I walk up to a guy and say I'm here with a Hertz car to get an oil change.

"Next door!" he yells over the sound of a screaming car alarm while jerking his thumb toward the next bay.

At the next bay I tell my story again, this time over the clatter of a pneumatic lug wrench, and again am given the thumb toward yet another bay westward, with the advice, "Ask for Eric!"

In the third bay, a guy with a nasty expression is sitting there, his feet stretched out comfortably, talking to one of the workers.

"Hi, I'm looking for Eric."

"Yeah?"

Yeah, I thought that was fairly clear. "Are you Eric?"

"Whaddya want?"

I have a flashback to the days when I was serving process. Either somebody's looking for this guy or he's just an unpleasant putz. "I have a Hertz car that needs an oil change. They said you folks can do it."

"Yeah, okay. Where is it?"

"Over there, at the curb."

"Bring it in."

"Well, the curb was about as close as I could get, but I guess I can go around the block." I figure I can make the loop and see if they'll make room for it if I approach the place from 26th, which is a one-way street heading east, which had prevented me from initially turning onto it.

"Yeah."

With that encouragement I head back to the car, but as I climb in another guy comes over and tells me to go back, he'll bring it around. So I walk back over to Mr. Sunshine and he tells me they'll have it done in twenty minutes to a half-hour and I can wait.

"I thought I'd leave it," I say, "and pick it up later. I have something to do uptown."

"Can't leave it. We got no room for it."

"Well, I'm afraid I can't wait, so what do you suggest we do?"

"When it's done I'll put it in the lot next door. Cost you twenty bucks."

"That seems a bit steep."

"How long'll you be?"

The interview is supposed to start at 12:30 and take twenty minutes, so I say, "I can be back by 1, maybe 1:30."

"Okay."

"Thanks," I say. "The information you'll need to contact Hertz is in the glove compartment."

"Yeah, yeah," and he turns away.

Refreshed by this pleasant exchange, I hail a cab and am dropped outside the 44th Street studio for Good Morning America Radio. This is, I had thought, to be one of the interviews that primarily focused on my friend John O'Donohue's book, *To Bless the Space Between Us*. John, a wonderful man—a former Catholic priest who had gone on to become a renowned poet and philosopher, an Irishman with a booming laugh, a great big heart and a silver-tongued brogue that could charm the birds from the trees—had died suddenly in January at the age of fifty-two. A stunning, heartbreaking loss to all of us who knew and loved him, his death came just as his new book was to be released, leaving this beautiful work orphaned, without this lovely man to introduce it to the world. So I and other friends agreed to try to help get the word out about it.

Beth Grossman, the book's publicist, has arranged a number of things for me to do in John's place, often generously trying to see to it that my own book is mentioned, though I'd assured her that wasn't necessary. And this is one of them. Or it was supposed to be. Meeting me outside, Beth tells me that the host of the show has read my book and wants to focus primarily on it, but will bring John and his book into the discussion.

This really isn't comfortable for me given our understanding, but Beth insists that she's happy with the agreement they have come to and urges me to go ahead with it. So I do. And it actually turns out very well. The host is smart, interesting, interested and very generous, not only about my book, but in the way she introduces John and his book into the conversation, weaving in our relationship and allowing me the chance to not only promote his book but to explain what a powerful influence he had become in my life. Among other things, I'm able to cite what he called his "unfinished poem": *I would love to live / like a river flows, / carried by the surprise / of its own unfolding.*

Ah, what a man. What a great loss. But I think we did him proud. And Beth was very pleased with the way it all went.

I take the subway down to 23rd Street and walk over to pick up Mule. She is done, parked on the street, and as I go to get the keys, Eric says, "That'll be forty bucks cash, no tax, no problem."

"That's to be taken care of by Hertz."

"Who says?"

"Well, I do, for one. That's what we talked about when I left the car."

"We didn't talk about nothin'. It's forty bucks."

"Look, pal," I say, feeling the heat rise, "maybe you misunderstood me awhile ago, but you got a call this morning explaining the situation and it was made clear that this is a Hertz car, that you folks have an agreement with Hertz, and that they'll pay for the oil change."

"I didn't get no call, so don't say I did nothin'. It's forty bucks."

Now I'm getting steamed. "Maybe we should get Hertz on the phone."

He doesn't like that. "You got a problem, talk to the man in there," he says, jerking his thumb toward yet another door into yet another bay.

I step through and find a little guy with a big belly on the phone. After a few minutes, he looks up at me and says, "Yeah?"

I explain the situation—rather calmly, I think.

"It's tough to get Hertz to pay, takes a long time."

"I'm sorry to hear that. But an agreement was made."

"You'll have to wait a few minutes then, cause right now I'm dealing with people who pay," and he returns to the phone.

I stand there, trying to think of what to do. I consider simply paying the money and arguing it out with Hertz at the end of the trip, but I can't let these creeps get away with this. I think about going back to Eric and grabbing the keys, walking out and taking the car—and, of course,

CENTER FOR CONSTITUTIONAL RIGHTS

The Center for Constitutional Rights is dedicated to advancing and protecting the rights guaranteed by the United States Constitution and the Universal Declaration of Human Rights. Founded in 1966 by attorneys who represented civil rights movements in the South, CCR is a nonprofit legal and educational organization committed to the creative use of law as a positive force for social change.

CCR uses litigation proactively to empower poor communities and communities of color to guarantee the rights of those with the fewest protections and least access to legal resources, and to train the next generation of civil and human rights attorneys.

Formed in order to work hand in hand with people's movements, CCR has lent its expertise and support to a wide range of movements for social justice. We are dedicated to defending the right to political dissent, combating the mass incarceration of both citizens and immigrants, and fighting government abuse of power. We strive to complete the unfinished civil rights movement through targeting racial profiling and other modern-day manifestations of racial and economic oppression, and through combating discrimination based on gender or sexuality.

dealing with whatever response that might prompt on his part. As I'm going through the various possibilities in my mind, this guy took yet another call. Standing there with the anger building, I can't help hearing what he's saying, which turns out to be about something he is using to deal with a health problem. It isn't working for him and it has to do with sleeping. As I pick up more words from his side of the conversation, it begins to sound like he is having trouble with a device he has to wear at night to treat sleep apnea, a condition a friend of mine suffers from. It's apparently very tough to deal with.

Hearing this, I'm thinking that maybe there's a better way to handle things. Maybe I can say something that'll put the two of us on a more human level and find a way to resolve this without turning it into a brawl. There's the chance, of course, that he'll object to my having overheard his private conversation and tell me to go fuck myself, but it's worth a thought, at least.

Just listening to him talk to the person on the other end of the phone

For decades, CCR has pushed U.S. courts to recognize international human rights and humanitarian protections—and we have had groundbreaking victories that have established the principle of universal jurisdiction in this country and extended human rights standards to abuses committed by corporations and other nongovernment groups. CCR also works to inform lawyers, policymakers, other organizations, and the public about ongoing legal and human rights violations.

CCR is currently engaged in several campaigns, including the 100 Days campaign, which focuses on the need to restore, protect, and expand the Constitution within the first 100 days of the next presidential administration. The campaign includes a series of white papers, videos, and a national speaking tour addressing key issues of ending torture and arbitrary detention, protecting the right to dissent, and rolling back executive power. CCR's Campaign for Telephone Justice won an historic victory in New York State, ending the prison telephone contract which charged the families of incarcerated people outrageous rates to maintain contact with their relatives. The Campaign for Telephone Justice is now working with other groups around the country, stressing the importance of maintaining family connections.

helps me lighten up a bit. He's clearly appreciative of the sympathetic hearing he's getting and gradually seems to be easier, less tough and abrasive.

Finally he hangs up, takes a deep breath and looks up at me.

"Sorry," I say. "I couldn't help but overhear. Sounds like sleep apnea?"

He nods.

"Friend of mine has had a hell of a time with it. I guess it's a bitch."

He gets up from the desk and comes around, saying he has to wear this device and he can't keep it on when asleep. "You stop breathing," he says, "until your brain wakes you up and tells you you gotta breathe. It's makin' me nuts."

"I'm sorry. That's got to be tough. But they're going to help?"

"Yeah, I think so." He pauses. "So where's your car?"

We go out, passing Eric, and I point to Mule.

"Has it been done yet?" he asks.

"I think so. They said it was."

We walk back in and he asks Eric, "Is it done?"

"Yeah."

He takes the key and we walk back out. He starts writing down the license number and other identifying information. I get him the rental agreement and we head back to his desk, again passing Eric, who says nothing.

As he sits back down and starts on the necessary papers, one of the workmen walks in behind me and says, "Hey, you Trapper John?"

"Nope. BJ."

"Hey, yeah, BJ! I love that show."

The guy at the desk now looks up and says, "You know, I thought you looked familiar. I watch that show every night."

"Yeah," the other guy says. "Where's Alan Alda?"

"He's out on Long Island, I think."

The guy at the desk says, "Farrell. Sure. Hell, I shoulda known. I thought you looked familiar!" Then he hands me the rental agreement. "Here. There's no reason to keep you here. I can take care of this."

"Are you sure? I don't want it to be a problem for you."

"Nah, no problem." He sticks out his hand. "Nice to meet you."

I shake his hand, thank him, shake the other guy's hand and walk out past Eric. I consider saying something to him, but then think, *Nah*.

Driving away with Mule, *MAINTENANCE* no longer *REQUIRED*, heading for an interview with my old friend David Bender on Air America, I find myself thinking that even though the message was a bit mixed—the big change coming with the realization that I was "somebody" in his mind—there was something happening even before that. I think I learned an important lesson back there.

Air America with David is a hoot. It's great to see him and be able to tear into America's bad guys a bit on the air. And when we're done I tape a short piece for the Center for Constitutional Rights about what President Obama should do in his first 100 days: close Guantánamo, end torture, end electronic spying (and lying), end the war in Iraq, join the International Criminal Court, open relations with Iran, end the embargo against Cuba, etc., etc. I also did a ninety-second rant against the death penalty on tape for Laura Flanders's new Dish Network TV and online show.

A rather productive afternoon.

In the evening, the *Nation* magazine and the Center for Constitutional Rights cosponsor an event at the Strand Bookstore in the Village, featuring yours truly and the wonderful writer Walter Mosley, talking about literature and politics and the future of this country.

I first met Walter when he accompanied Edwidge Danticat, the powerful young Hatian writer, around the Brooklyn Book Festival in 2007.

We next saw each other at Harry Belafonte's "Gathering for Justice" for young activists in Oakland, California. Sharing the podium with such a talented man, a serious and accomplished author, was more than a bit intimidating for this neophyte, but Walter was charming, gracious and more than generous. I found him to be a very bright guy with a skeptic's eye and a sardonic wit. He's always ready with a challenge and is in serious danger of becoming a friend.

The discussion is moderated by an articulate woman named Annette Dickerson, an officer of the CCR, who had stepped in because Michael Ratner, who heads the organization and was scheduled to handle it, had been called away. Annette told me that she had read and loved my book, which is nice to hear. But then she makes a point of telling me again, which is even nicer. Coming back to the subject later, she says, "I cried when I read it. I cried when I read about 'The House.' I wish there were places like that for everyone."

I wish there were as well.

Some old friends are in the audience. Al Ruben, a highly regarded veteran who wrote the script for *Incident at Dark River,* a clumsily titled (not our choice) movie my partner and I produced, surprised me by showing up. And in the front row is a pal, the always-sassy Alysse Minkoff, who, having survived serious challenges in life, is making sure she misses nothing. Years ago, after reading of my adventures in Bosnia, Alysse decided she had to go there and do what she could to help—and did. And here she is again, not only showing up and being supportive, but accompanied by two lovely friends who pay close attention and seem to enjoy themselves as well.

Perfectly in character, Alysse is now taking New York by storm—but that's yet another story.

DAY NINETEEN

Wednesday, May 28, 2008

CITY OF ORIGIN: NEW YORK, NY

MILES TRAVELED: 372

CITY OF DESTINATION: PITTSBURGH, PA

VENUE: JOSEPH-BETH BOOKSELLERS

EVENT COSPONSOR

ACLU of Pennsylvania

U p early for an interview this morning, an Iowa paper interested in my upcoming visit. Today Mule and I will head west, beginning to close the big circle.

Interview done, I go get Mule, who is hobbled in an underground stall two blocks away, this being New York City, then load up and try to figure out how to get out of town. The directions take us through concrete canyons and right up to what I now recognize as Ground Zero. We'd passed it before, but I hadn't grasped its significance, thinking it was simply another huge construction project. Seeing it now, remembering the horror, the pictures of panicked people running through these very streets in the dust and smoke, trying to escape from the collapsing buildings, remembering the bodies falling . . . to be there is . . . hard to put into words, but deeply moving.

But back to here and now, on this route the cars are fighting for inches. Traffic is a monstrous, groaning caterpillar that moves like glue. A fire engine turns into the street ahead of us, blaring its siren and honking its horn, but it's almost impossible for those in front of it to get out of the way. Progress, such as it is, slows even more.

Finally, a block away from the street my directions tell me I need to get to, we're stopped by police and directed away. The fire, it appears, is on that block. The mess here is insane. At this rate I'll still be trying to find my way out of Manhattan when the people show up at the bookstore in Pittsburgh tonight.

And then, magic happens. For all the embarrassment I sometimes feel from the special, if unwarranted treatment the impact of having been part of *M*A*S*H* can bring my way, it can once in a while seem heaven-sent. Diverted from the street the directions call for, Mule and I are in a sea of frustration with drivers honking, swearing and maneuvering for advantage, and I have no clue which way to go. Movement to my right gets my attention and I see it's a police car, so roll down the window and yell across to the officer, "How do I get to the Holland Tunnel?"

He points straight ahead and says, "Get on the Westside Highway," then turns away.

Okay, so we'll wade through this mess until . . . And a horn honks beside me. The same cop, now smiling, yells, "You still acting?"

I call back, "Sure. Once in a while."

He turns to say something to the guy beside him, then turns back and yells, "Turn here!" pointing to his right. He stops to let me by and I turn, then he races around and signals me to follow him. In a flash, with Mule on his tail, we move around lines of cars, making quick rights and lefts.

"This is very cool!" I shout to Mule, but then it occurs to me that maybe I misunderstood and he'll look back, see us, pull over and say, "What the hell do you think you're doing?"

But no. After one more corner he pulls over, waves us up beside him, points straight ahead and says with a smile, "Go to the end and turn right. Once you get to Canal Street, follow the signs." I yell my thanks, he gives a thumbs-up and we're off. Suddenly we're on the Westside Highway and in a few minutes going through the Holland Tunnel.

What a guy. God bless him. And thank you *M*A*S*H*!

Through the tunnel the signs are confusing and I'm sure we've made the wrong turn, but at least we're in New Jersey, so I'll figure it out. A few miles down the road it's suddenly clear that it wasn't the wrong turn at all; we're just where we ought to be. These signs are crazy-making.

Racing westward, we're soon out of the ugly industrial part of New Jersey, the oil refinery, junkyard part that brings to mind bodies, their feet encased in cement, at the bottom of deep water. The bright green forests, rolling hills and quiet communities that now appear run counter to the popular image of the state. I remember how surprised I was to find this beautiful New Jersey many years ago when my partner Marvin and I met with the writer J.P. Miller *(Days of Wine and Roses)* at his home in one of these rural communities. Nice man, J.P. Too bad we couldn't get that project off the ground.

It's a long drive to Pittsburgh, lots of time to think.

Passing a number of dead deer at the side of the road brings a pang. Even in death they bespeak innocence and grace. There's something about these shy, beautiful, harmless creatures with the life smashed out of them by onrushing, unfeeling machinery that seems a metaphor for what is too often lost in the pell-mell "advance of civilization."

Looking out at the simplicity and grandeur of the tree-covered mountains makes me think again of the Native Americans who roamed this area before our arrival, living off the land, yet living with it. Lucky, aren't they, that we've been able to teach them so much?

New Jersey leads to Pennsylvania, less aggressively green but still beautiful. More tree-covered rolling hills here, but a softer contour to it as they give way to farmland.

Passing through Amish country brings to mind the stunning, heart-breaking, awe-inspiring dignity of the Amish community when dealing with the horrifying murder of so many of their children those many months ago. Their grief palpable, the pain unimaginable, they embraced one another, took solace in their faith and remained unwilling to stoop to a vengeful response.

So much to learn, so much to know.

Arriving in Pittsburgh, the town is crazed. The hotel, directly across the street from Mellon Arena, is a zoo. The Penguins ("The Pens" to the locals) are in the Stanley Cup playoffs. Down two games to the Detroit Red Wings, both games having been played in Detroit, they're competing here tonight and tensions are sky-high. I'm barely able to fight my way through the crowds to find a place for Mule and get into my room. Hockey fans are everywhere. If the Pens can't take advantage of "home ice," the bellman tells me, it's all over, so the fever is high.

After a quick change Mule carts me down to Joseph-Beth Booksellers on the South Side. I'm excited to be back there because it's where we shot *Dominick and Eugene* just over twenty years ago. The store is in a new, upscale section of South Side, just east of and quite different from the funky, down-home areas we shot in. But it still has that comfortable Pittsburgh feeling.

The crowd at the bookstore is much smaller than I've been finding at these events, testifying to Pittsburgh's devotion to the Pens. Chris and Maureen, the managers of the store, are a bit embarrassed, I think, but they're certainly not to blame. Who knew that such a critical game would take place tonight? Who knew, in fact, that the Pens would be vying for the championship? Good on them.

Despite their number, the group that has come is every bit as attentive and interested as have been the others. The group actually grows in size as the evening goes on and we end up, I think, having a good time. I certainly did.

My friend Marshall Dayan was sweet enough to come and bring his pal Mark, a former journalist who has become a respected poet. Marshall, a capital-case criminal defense specialist, came to Pittsburgh last year to join the Federal Public Defender's office after working for many years in the South—Georgia and North Carolina. This move to the North is more than a change in climate, it puts him into a different mindset. A former chair of the National Coalition to Abolish the Death Penalty, Marshall is highly respected, not to mention deeply loved, in the anti–capital punishment community and was responsible for my making the keynote speech here at an ACLU death penalty conference last March.

After I've said my piece and we've done the Q&A, books are signed and pictures are taken. People are so incredibly sweet in these brief, sort of private moments. One young couple knocks me out by saying they've driven here from DC today because they missed seeing me when I was there the other day! Sometimes it's hard to comprehend the connection people make with the show, but I'm always touched by it.

Marshall and Mark agree to join me for dinner at Café Allegro, a wonderful restaurant on 12th Street in Bedford Square where we shot much of *Dominick and Eugene*. Antoinette, the proprietor, was so kind and generous to us during the shooting of the film that I wanted to be sure to stop in and see if she's still there. She is, as it turns out, and as sweet and open and generous as ever. The place has expanded and the food is as good as I remember. After we talk for a while, Antoinette disappears for a few minutes and comes back with a big paste-up that she's kept in her office, full of pictures and articles from the time we were here.

She talks about "the boys," Tom Hulce and Ray Liotta, who played the twins, and clucks over a photo of Jamie Lee Curtis with the baby.

Sitting there surrounded by happy memories from the picture, I'm reminded of a problem that developed. Needing a baby for an important story point in the picture, we had cast local twins, whose parents were thrilled to have them be part of it. But just as we were getting ready to start shooting, someone told us there was a law in Pennsylvania prohibiting children under six from working.

We were stunned. Certainly we understood an opposition to "child labor" and the need to protect kids from being abused, but this was a movie. We needed a baby!

After going over all the possibilities, which included packing up and finding another state in which to shoot the picture, I asked if anyone knew Harris Wofford, an old friend of mine who had briefly been a U.S. Senator from Pennsylvania. Harris and I met through our mutual friendship with Al Lowenstein, another mythic figure in American politics, and grew to be friends. Yes, came the reply, he's still involved in politics here in the state.

"Really? What does he do?"

"He's the Minister of Labor."

I couldn't believe it! After a series of calls I finally reached him and explained the situation. He said, "I'll be there tomorrow." And he was.

We had dinner together right here at Café Allegro and worked out the necessary permit process to allow us to go forward with the film, with the baby.

What a wonderful time that was. And what a lovely picture came of it.

Back at the hotel, as I'm preparing to tuck in at the end of the night, a very loud burst of fireworks tells me that the Pens have taken the game before their home crowd and are still in the hunt.

DAY TWENTY
Thursday, May 29, 2008

CITY OF ORIGIN: PITTSBURGH, PA

MILES TRAVELED: 291

CITY OF DESTINATION: ANN ARBOR, MI

VENUE: BARNES & NOBLE—ANN ARBOR

EVENT COSPONSOR
ACLU of Michigan

U p early again, this time for a terrific interview with Jim Rice of WCCO radio in Minneapolis. A true journalist, Rice has just returned from Darfur. He's been to Iraq, Kosovo, the West Bank, Gaza and other hot spots and doesn't back off from letting his audience know about what's happening. Off the air, Rice tells me he's a former CIA agent and is not a fan of current U.S. foreign policy. When I tell him of my visit with Joe Wilson and Valerie Plame, it touches a nerve. He's outraged by the Bush administration's having outed Valerie, a NOC (nonofficial cover) agent. They are the ones, he says, who are under the deepest cover without any official support to fall back on if discovered. To betray her for political gain, as they did, is beneath contempt. I like this guy.

Pittsburgh is calm this morning. Evidently the celebrators are sleeping it off. The game was hard fought, but the Pens took it 3 to 2.

Hitting the interstate, we're up for another long drive. I'd love to do this kind of round-the-nation trip on my motorcycle some time, but the interstates are murder when you're on a bike, exhausting, boring and dangerous. The little roads where you can see and smell and taste the country are where the fun is. Cross-country bike trips are therapy for me and I've done them in different parts of the world. But for a trip like this, with limited time and a need to cover big distances between stops, the interstates that stripe the country are a necessity. And Mule is doing wonderfully, still sailing past the gas stations while eating up the miles. The only thing she's beeped at me about lately is when we stop and I forget to pull out that hunk of plastic that pretends to be an ignition key.

Passing into Ohio, the driving becomes automatic. Can't deal with the radio today. Rush, Sean and the Rush/Sean wannabes and troglodytes continue to spew their versions of Roger Ailes's daily right-wing talking points. Those guys are organized, I'll give 'em that.

But who needs the radio? I talk to Mule, talk to myself, talk to other drivers, read signs out loud, sing. I'm a regular circus. People used to say talking to yourself was okay, but if you answered you were nuts. If that's true, I'm gone. I not only talk to myself and answer, I say funny things to myself and make myself laugh.

The mind wanders . . .

You know, those of us who drive the freeways, highways and interstates are used to seeing semis carting products around the country. But did you ever think of counting them? There are millions of the things! And it makes me think about the economy. I know we're in a slump now, one that Bush won't admit is a recession, but the economic engine is still strong, it just needs the kind of leadership these "free marketeers" won't provide. I heard a kid on right-wing radio the other day saying that the unemployment rate was "only" five percent. Aside from the fact that the number they currently tout ignores thousands who have given up and are thus no longer factored in the calculation, how is it that having five percent of our employable workforce unable to get jobs is an "only?" How is it acceptable at all? Whatever happened to the idea of full employment?

These semis are doing important work, but they're chewing up the roads and putting more and more stress on our bridges. Remember Minnesota? The infrastructure in this country is in need of serious attention, and the money to do it, instead of creating a major government-funded jobs program, is being wasted on a mindless, destructive crusade in Iraq.

Did you happen to notice the picture on the front page of Wednesday's *New York Times*? A Chinese government official is on his knees, imploring the people of his community to give up the protest against their leaders. The people were enraged by the poor construction of the schools in which their children were crushed when they collapsed in the earthquake. Quite a picture. George Bush and Dick Cheney should have been on their knees to the people of New Orleans after the failure of the levees. But no, Bush was swaggering and smirking at a fundraiser with John McCain while Cheney was snorting derisively in an undisclosed location.

The Chinese government, however we might despise their human rights record, stepped up after this catastrophic earthquake, not only sending reconstruction teams and experts, not only allowing in international aid organizations, but dispatching over 100,000 troops to the disaster area to dig people out. Why didn't Cheney and Bush send 100,000 troops to New Orleans to rescue people and rebuild their homes? Because they were in Iraq, destroying a nation.

Cheney and Bush, along with Rove, Wolfowitz, Feith, Rumsfeld,

Bolton, Abrams, and the rest of their gang should be stripped naked and made to walk through every city, town and village that has lost a son or daughter in this criminal war and be bathed in the vilification and opprobrium they so richly deserve.

And what about Scott McClellan, who I always thought of as Bush's own Pillsbury Doughboy? Think the revelations in his new book are giving them fits? Good to have some inside information, at long last, but how does McClellan justify spilling it all now to make a buck after toeing the line—promoting the line—while all those kids died?

Enough . . . I'm getting dyspepsia.

Skimming across the top of Ohio, the map tells me we're skirting the southern edge of Lake Erie. Amazing. From Los Angeles' Pacific Ocean down to the Mexican border at El Paso, the Gulf of Mexico at New Orleans, through the southeast, up to New York on the Atlantic, and now heading west across the top of the U.S.! One hell of a trip this Mule has carted me on, and we're not even two-thirds of the way around yet.

Crossing into Michigan, we get to Ann Arbor in time for me to find a very good vegetarian restaurant—Seva, if you're in the neighborhood—and have dinner before the event at the Barnes & Noble on the east side of town.

Once there, the event manager meets me at the door and asks if it's true that Shelley's not with me. When I say it is, she says she heard Shelley fell and broke her hip.

"How did you hear that?" I ask, a bit taken aback.

"Someone in the group waiting for you told me. She read about it."

Oh my God. Does that mean someone's actually reading this thing? I take it all back.

The crowd upstairs is quite large and very friendly. I note that a group of young kids are taking notes. Later, one of them says their teacher is a "big fan" and made being here and reporting on my remarks a class assignment. Thanks, teach.

Lots of laughs tonight.

After a stop at the Whole Foods next door, we beat it back to the hotel to cheer the Lakers on to victory in the Western Conference. The Spurs had me worried for a while, but here come the glory days!

DAY TWENTY-ONE

Friday, May 30, 2008

CITY OF ORIGIN: ANN ARBOR, MI

MILES TRAVELED: 445

CITY OF DESTINATION: IOWA CITY, IA

VENUE: PRAIRIE LIGHTS BOOKSTORE

EVENT COSPONSOR

Peace, Education, and Action Center of Eastern Iowa (PEACE Iowa)

Before we hit the road, Mule needs some oats. This is the first time on this trip I've paid $4 or more per gallon. This time it was either $4.12 or $4.21, I can't remember which. I think it was $4.12, but either is too much. Michigan is being hit hard—in a lot of ways.

Heading west on the interstate again, I find myself thinking about a couple of the comments from last night. A man asked me if it was true that Shelley had starred in a movie with Elvis Presley. When I told him that in fact Shelley is the only actress to have starred in not one but three movies with Elvis, a woman called out, "Does that make you jealous?"

I said, "Nope. He's dead, you know."

Shelley is dearly loved. We talked about "Johnny Angel" after one man passed around a copy of the cover from a CD of one of her albums. There was talk of *Coach* and *The Donna Reed Show,* and later a young woman gave me a card to pass on to her.

It's lovely that so many have such warm feelings for her. I do too.

Driving through the Michigan farmland I try the radio again and get a local talk show. The host is speaking about the tough economic times here in Michigan and says they're considering a four-day work week (four ten-hour days) to cut down on commuting costs. Some study has suggested people will save thousands of dollars a year by simply eliminating that one driving day from their week.

There's much talk about the price of gasoline, the rising cost of groceries and stagnant wages. A local car dealer is having a promotion that involves a giveaway of groceries and gas coupons. Hmmm. Gas coupons as an incentive to buy a gas guzzler?

Interesting, too, that amid the discussion of bad economic times there's mention of a rash of arrests having to do with the discovery of a series of meth labs. Tough times tend to create both a need to escape and a way to make some easy money. Sad.

Weather report warns of possible "flooding rains," thunder storms and hail, plus a tornado watch. Noting that the skies are looking pretty unfriendly up ahead of us, I listen closely. Except for some rain in New Mexico and Texas, we've been pretty lucky on this trip. I do remember, though, that in Austin they had had a major hailstorm a few days before we got there. The woman who hosted the fundraiser there said huge hailstones had broken seventeen windows in her house.

This report says that the bad weather is expected in this area tonight or tomorrow. Today it's in Iowa. Lovely. Iowa City is where we're headed.

The radio guy says the police have endorsed a petition by a group of motorcyclists asking that they be allowed to file for permits that will allow them to ride without helmets. What kind of nonsense is that? And why would the police support it? Then he says the fee charged for the permits would go to the police budget. Ah. Fine. Let these guys get their brains splattered all over the road so you can have more cops to pick up the pieces? Nuts.

Bulletin: tornado damage reported in Iowa.

Oh boy . . .

This weekend is the big Democratic Party conference that's to decide the fate of the Michigan and Florida delegations to the convention. That should be interesting. I don't understand—well, I guess I do understand, but it seems to me the height of hypocrisy—how Hillary can insist that the full delegations from Florida and Michigan be seated and allowed to cast their votes for her when 1) Obama's name wasn't even on the Michigan ballot, 2) both had agreed not to campaign in either state, 3) the votes came early, before Obama's campaign caught fire and it was assumed Hillary was the nominee, and 4) both had agreed, along with everyone else, that neither state's delegation would be seated because they had violated the rules established by the party before the primaries.

Well, I guess we'll see what they decide . . .

Down we go, into Indiana, and then cut west toward Des Moines. It's starting to rain a bit, but not bad. The wind is blowing like hell, which has Mule a bit skittish, and there are more reports of tornadoes, but I don't see anything that looks dangerous. Chicago, which is now north of us, is broadcasting storm warnings.

I keep trying to compute the miles we've traveled based on notes I've made in order to figure out how far we have left to go, but I think I'm getting stupid from too much driving or too little sleeping, or both. I keep coming up with different numbers. I'm looking for exit 244, and I think it's in this leg, but I've got a 207-mile leg and a 168-mile leg and my brain is getting fried.

Wow! Cops have the left lane blocked off. This highway is divided by a wide grassy median that slopes down from each side in a kind of V shape with a trough at the bottom. It looks like the wind got to be too much for a semi and a big RV, as they are both down in the bottom of the trough. The two are upright, which is good, but judging from the tracks, the semi driver had to wrestle that sucker around to keep it from going over. It appears that no one is hurt, but it looks muddy down there, so some big tow trucks are working their way down to pull them out. This wind is tough enough on Mule; I'd hate to be driving one of those rigs in it.

Whoa, whoa, whoa! I'm on Highway 80 West, have been for what seems like hours, looking for exit 244, and have just realized the numbers of the exits are going DOWN. They're getting smaller, not larger! How can that be? Des Moines is still ahead of us and I don't know how many miles we've traveled in Iowa, but this doesn't make sense. I grab the almanac and try to read it while keeping Mule on the road. From what I can see with a quick glance, Iowa City is not far into the state. Does that mean I drove right past the turnoff?

Idiot! I'm completely baffled. How could I have missed it? How far back is it? How much time is left before I have to be there?

Spotting an exit, I get off, but quickly see it's another highway with nowhere to stop. Shit! I'm starting to panic. How the hell . . . ? Finally, I find an exit and pull off so I can stop. This is Highway 39. Where the hell is Highway 39 on the map? Can't find it. But sure as hell, Iowa City, where I'm supposed to be going, is quite near the eastern border of Iowa. I must have driven right by it while my brain was somewhere else. I'll have to double back. But something keeps telling me this makes no sense.

I head back toward the highway, then stop again. Something's wrong. There are a few buildings not too far off the highway, I'll check there and see if they can help me. I turn around, drive down, pull into what looks like a big tractor garage and get out. A woman is leaving the place and I ask her how to get to Iowa City. She turns to a man in the garage, who says, "Go back down to Highway 80."

Right, I get that, that's the road I was on.

He says, "It's west of here, probably three to four hours."

It's west of here? How the hell can it be west of here? According to the map it's only a little way into the state. But I nod, like an idiot, and say, "80 and west?"

He says, "Right."

"Okay," I say, "thanks."

Pulling away, my head is spinning. This makes no sense at all. The exit numbers are going down, not up. How can exit 244 be west of here? How can it be three or four hours west of here if it's not far from the eastern . . . ? Oh shit! I stop again, pull out the almanac, look at the map of Iowa. Then I burst out laughing.

"You're not in Iowa, you fucking idiot! You're in Illinois."

Oh man, oh man, oh man! I sit there and laugh and laugh and laugh. The miles and the driving and the wind and the rain and the map and the exit numbers and the calculations and the time change . . . I have completely lost it. I need to go to sleep.

Heading back down to Highway 80 and then on west through the rest of ILLINOIS, I'm grinning like a fool. What a relief! Every once in a while I burst out laughing again.

Sure enough, once actually in Iowa it's not far to Iowa City and the hotel. The bad weather seems to have blown north. There are reports of tornadoes and damage in the Chicago area, but there's been no sign of bad weather since I figured out what state I was in. There's even a natural food restaurant near the hotel and I have time to eat before I report to the Prairie Lights Bookstore, which is within walking distance from the hotel. Ain't it grand how some things work out?

After dinner and a change, I head over. Just outside the hotel there's a big plaza area with a band playing. Hundreds of people of all ages are sitting around enjoying the show. Shades of the Pens, I have competition tonight.

Prairie Lights is a nice store, not small but not awfully large, and there's only one fellow behind the counter in front and two in back waiting on one customer. Uh oh . . . The fellow in front sends me to the rear, saying, "You'd better go up the back way, there's not too much room up there."

Upstairs, I turn a corner and am startled to find a huge crowd that erupts into applause when I appear. Man, this is not what I expected at all! The room is full to bursting, with all the seats occupied, people on the floor, in the aisles and many more standing. I'm simply knocked out.

Julie Englander, the owner of the store, has set this up as part of a regular broadcast she does on a local NPR station, *Live from Prairie Lights*. Unlike most of the events I've been doing, this is relatively formal, circumscribed as it is by time because of the broadcast, so Julie acts as the moderator to keep things moving along. But even though it's not the free-flowing format I'm used to, the evening seems to go very well. The people, once we get to the Q&A session (which is what I like best), are so incredibly sweet it's embarrassing. They keep thanking me for coming and expressing support and appreciation for what I've been doing. The embrace that *M*A*S*H* continues to enjoy is stunning—and deeply moving.

Once the "show" is over things loosen up a bit, with people lining up to have me sign books and take pictures. Julie sets down some sheets for me to sign that can be pasted into books later, explaining that they've already sold out of the ones on hand.

This is really amazing! I like Iowa—once I found it, that is.

Questions and lovely comments keep coming until everything is signed and all the pictures are done. Just near the end of the line, a sweet young woman comes up and identifies herself as the daughter of a very old friend of mine, one I actually mentioned in the book. He has, I learned only last year, passed away, and because we'd lost touch, I've not met his family. She asks me to sign a book for her and another for her brother, and then, after we talk for a bit, she waits around until everyone else is gone and approaches me again. Very shyly, she asks if I would be willing to talk to her at another time. She doesn't really know much about her father, she says, and would very much like to learn about him.

"How old were you when he died?"

"Six."

Oh Jesus. The heart breaks. I held her for a moment and gave her my numbers. Then I hugged her again, saying, "I look forward to talking to you. Your father was a good man."

Later, I head for the hotel pondering the amazing things that have happened on this trip. Thinking about Bud and his daughter . . . well, even if for no other reason, the entire adventure has now been worthwhile . . .

DAY TWENTY-TWO

Saturday, May 31, 2008

CITY OF ORIGIN: IOWA CITY, IA

MILES TRAVELED: 304

CITY OF DESTINATION: MINNEAPOLIS, MN

VENUE: MAGERS & QUINN BOOKSELLERS

EVENT COSPONSORS

Center for Victims of Torture, Minnesota Democratic-Farmer-Labor Veterans Caucus

Turns out I was wrong. When I stop into Prairie Lights this morning to pick up a copy of the *New York Times,* I find that Julie Englander, who hosted the show last night, is not the owner of the store, but rather a producer for the local PBS station who regularly does her show here.

Got a late start this morning, so missed the chance to meet with Jean Hessburg, an old friend who lives a couple of hours away and couldn't make it last night. We had hoped for time to connect this morning, but I have to be in Minneapolis for a late-afternoon event, so it won't work.

A terrific woman, Jean was involved in Democratic politics here in Iowa and then transplanted to California some years ago. She had worked with a number of Iowa politicos and was put in touch with us by Senator Tom Harkin or former Congressman Dave Nagle—maybe both. She landed on her feet in California, becoming an organizer and spokesperson for Norman Lear's group, People for the American Way.

I remember watching in awe as she deftly debated a group of Christian fundamentalists who were trying to insinuate their religious views into the school curriculum in an outlying Southern California community.

Having returned to Iowa, she was back working for the Democratic Party for a while—one of her jobs being to organize the Nevada caucuses. I'm sorry to miss the chance to catch up.

Filling the tank before heading north to Minnesota, I calculate that Mule is getting over fifty miles per gallon. Damn, that's impressive.

The radio tells me that a study finds that 75 million out of 100 million American workers say they're burned out on their jobs. Think we have some problems in this country?

Beautiful, clear day here in Iowa. Blue sky dotted with fluffy white clouds. None of that tornado talk, I'm happy to say.

This is a gorgeous state. It's quite flat, full of farms and neatly tended land. The homes we pass, the barns, the fields, all have a clean, well-cared-for appearance. Very Norman Rockwell, this American heartland.

Racing along the highway I see lots and lots of motorcycles, mostly traveling in large groups. Yesterday there were guys sporting insignia identifying them as military veterans, today it just looks like clubs, but none of them appear to be the "outlaw" types. Just people out for a ride on a beautiful day. I can certainly understand that, though riding in a pack is not my style.

For me it's a solitary, meditative pleasure. And, I must say, I'm not a fan of the big Harley-types I see on the road so often. To each his own, of course, but I like a bike that's lighter and easier to handle, made to go off on a dirt road or up a mountain trail if one looks tempting. If you try something like that on one of those big Hogs and happen to go down, you'll need three men and a crane to pick it up again.

I don't know why I'm surprised to find them here in northeast Iowa, but we're passing through an open field full of electricity-generating windmills, those graceful spires with triangular propellers reminiscent of the prop on the old World War II fighter planes. What is it about this place? Even these things look particularly elegant here.

Passing into southern Minnesota I begin to see signs announcing familiar-sounding towns. My mother was born in a small town that's probably not far from here: Millville, Minnesota. One of ten kids raised primarily by their mother—my grandfather having been killed when Mom was seven—she never spoke of being "poor," but her stories suggested a pretty hardscrabble life for all of them. She never complained, but it was always clear to us that she didn't want to see anything wasted, part of the legacy of that experience. And she was never comfortable with the sort of lifestyle so many of us take for granted, full of what I'm sure she saw as excess.

DAMN!! Everything can change in a split second. A car in the right lane about five lengths ahead of us slams on its brakes, the rear end lifts, fishtails to the right, to the left, back again, almost flips and then shoots left, straight across both lanes and into the grassy median, down, up the other side, spins around and rolls backward before finally coming to a stop. Meanwhile, cars are swerving all over the place to avoid hitting him and each other. It's a miracle there isn't a tremendous pile-up.

I'm able to put on the flashers and pull Mule over onto the grass so that people can get by, then check to see if he's okay. He is, though clearly shaken up. I can't see anyone else in the car and he says he's alone. He gets out swearing, walks around a bit saying the guy in front of him slammed on his brakes. I didn't see that, but if he did, this guy must have been following too closely or just not paying attention. He has a phone; he doesn't want help. It's clear he's embarrassed, so once I'm sure he'll be able to handle it, Mule and I take off.

Damn. So close. Split seconds . . .

As we come into Minneapolis, the sky is beginning to cloud over again while we find the hotel and get situated. A very chi-chi place, the Graves 601 Hotel, apparently where the "in-crowd" gathers. Not my cup of tea, exactly, but it's hard to complain about the extra comforts, especially when I've been pretty much living out of a car for the past three weeks. The way some live stays on my mind, though, as Mule and I quickly head out under a threatening sky to Magers & Quinn Booksellers for today's event, this one cosponsored by the Center for Victims of Torture.

I spoke there last year and have known people associated with it for some years. Impressive place. The first of its kind in the U.S., the Center was founded here in Minneapolis in 1985 and has offices in St. Paul and Washington, DC, plus "healing centers" in Sierra Leone, Liberia and the Democratic Republic of Congo.

Despite the clever attempts at wordplay by Bush/Cheney apologists and the cowardly tap dancing of our new attorney general, "water boarding" is torture.

It's infuriating beyond my capacity to fully express it—even when giving myself leave to use the most vile words I can think of—to know that our own country has stooped to the level of torturing human beings under this vicious gang of thugs propping up George W. Bush.

Nearing the block where the Magers & Quinn bookstore is located, I find the street closed for a fair of some kind. Traffic is snarled and parking is impossible. I finally find a spot a couple of blocks away and walk to the store to find a Beer Festival covering the whole block, complete with loud music and a huge crowd of beered-up kids dancing in the street.

Not, I suspect, an atmosphere conducive to a book event, even assuming people wanting to come can fight their way through the traffic and find a place to park. Oh well . . .

Inside, it appears I'm right. Ten or fifteen people are sitting in the space they've set aside for the event, and the manager, a bit embarrassed, apologizes. They evidently had no advance notice—or perhaps not enough—to do anything about it, but he remains hopeful and asks if I'd mind waiting awhile to allow time for others who might have been delayed by the mess outside.

After a bit, with the group now maybe twice the size it was when I came in, we go ahead. Despite the relatively small crowd, they're kind, thoughtful and interested, and they ask good questions, so we have fun. One of the group, it turns out, is a distant cousin, Kevin Geraghty, who has been assiduously compiling a family history. He's brought his wife and son, and I believe they've driven in from quite a distance away. Kevin and my brother Jim, who has been doing a lot of investigating along the same line, have had an ongoing exchange of information. As it turns out, Jim is due here in town in a couple of weeks and they're going

CENTER FOR VICTIMS OF TORTURE

The Center for Victims of Torture (CVT) is an international leader in providing care and rehabilitative services to survivors of torture by extending hope and healing to survivors. In 1985, CVT was established as the first organization of its kind in the U.S., and only the third in the world, after careful study by a special task force convened by Minnesota Governor Rudy Perpich. Today, CVT works locally, nationally, and internationally to build healing communities where torture survivors feel welcomed, protected, and healed. Our programs are divided into four areas: client services, training, research, and public policy and education.

Our client services focus is on helping survivors in Minnesota and in Africa. In two Twin Cities locations, CVT provides rehabilitative services to more than 250 survivors each year, as well as information/referral services to an additional 100 survivors. In centers in Liberia, Sierra Leone, and the Democratic Republic of Congo, CVT clinicians

to get together and pick each other's brains. Nice man, Kevin. Nice of him to show up.

After books are signed and pictures taken, I'm greeted by Nancy Gertner, Associate Chair of the Democratic-Farm-Labor Veterans Caucus, a group of vets from Vietnam and Iraq who are angry about this war, the way veterans are being treated, and intent on doing what they can to bring about change. Nancy had contacted me through Johanna when they heard I was coming to town and asked if I'd meet with them.

As we wrap up at Magers & Quinn and head out to meet the vets, the sky opens up. It is a spectacular display, so we stand there under the shop's awning and watch a downpour of hail that looks like God has emptied out a huge barrel of marbles. It's amazing, the kind of thing that if you saw it in a movie you'd think it overdone. Pummeling those crazy or drunk enough to be out there running around or dancing in it, bouncing off everything and gathering on every level surface, these good-sized ice marbles make a fabulous show. I am glad we are protected by the awning and keep checking to see that it's holding.

Finally, it stops and the crowd gives a huge cheer just as a beautiful

offer mental health counseling to nearly 2,500 victims of torture, and train members of the affected population to be psychosocial peer counselors (PSCs).

As a leader in torture-survivor rehabilitation, CVT trains health, education, and human services professionals who work with torture survivors and refugees in the U.S. and around the globe. In doing so, we are also able to conduct research on the most effective torture-survivor treatment methods. While we work to heal the wounds of torture, we hope for a day when our efforts are no longer necessary. So CVT collaborates with local, national, and international organizations on public education, policy, and advocacy initiatives aimed at the prevention and ultimate elimination of torture.

CVT relies on donations to promote healing of torture survivors. Individuals can also influence torture-related policy by communicating with their elected officials and participating in our e-mail advocacy campaigns.

rainbow spreads across the sky. Nancy says she thinks they're cheering the rainbow. I kind of figure they're happy about being able to go back to the drinking and dancing.

Meeting the vets, an angry and spirited group, I hear about two Iraq veterans they have already elected to Congress and about two more—Ashwin Madia and Steve Sarvi—whom they're intending to put there by knocking off two sitting Republicans. Madia, a lawyer, worked on establishing a system of law in Iraq. Sarvi, who comes in as we're talking, is a very bright, articulate guy who was frustrated at every step in Iraq. His superiors wanted him to build some useless facilities to play up to the local authorities. He wanted to build schools, so did. He also tells me that he had tried to dissuade the Iraqi police and military from torturing those they captured. He said they had a special room, lined with tile like a shower—but no showerhead—where they took prisoners and worked them over. He said that when he tried to explain to the Iraqis that this stuff was not only illegal but counterproductive, they'd say, "Really? Tell me about water boarding." As he says, you can't win that argument. You can't tell them not to do something when they know that you're doing it all the time.

We all swap stories for quite awhile. I don't know how much good I am able to do them, but I am sure impressed with their energy. Hope for the future!

Later, walking out into the cold Minnesota night, I find a quiet restaurant and have a nice dinner. Heading back by a different route, I am hailed on a lonely stretch of a dark street by a homeless man. I'm always frustrated by these approaches because I don't want to be insensitive to the need, but, concerned that any money I hand over will only be spent on booze or drugs, I also don't want to be a chump. However, something about this guy touches me, so I listen to his story. He is in from out of town, he says, needs a place to sleep and, having found the shelters full, is trying to raise enough money for a cheap motel room to get out of the cold. He is truly embarrassed to be asking, he says, but simply has no choice.

How many times have I heard this story or one like it? But something . . . something about this awful situation—me headed to a warm bed and him reduced to this state—makes me think, *What the hell?* When I hand him the money he looks at it, does a double-take, and exclaims, "Oh my God! Thank you! I can get a room!" As I wish him well and move away, he comes after me, thanking me profusely and insisting that I give him an address so he can return the money when he gets back on his feet. I tell him it isn't necessary and say good night, but he begs me to let him prove he isn't lying.

Finally, I figure *What the hell?* again, give him a business card, shake his hand and head back to my chi-chi hotel for the night. Mom would not have liked the place.

(And you know, six months later I get a letter from Billy. He wants me to know that he's working at a mission, serving his brothers and sisters and doing well. Our meeting that night, he writes, was the beginning of a turning point for him and he sends God's blessings.)

DAY TWENTY-THREE

Sunday, June 1, 2008

CITY: MINNEAPOLIS, MN

OFF DAY

A day off! Not due in Sioux Falls until tomorrow night, I've been given a day of leisure here in the Twin Cities.

Mule and I go over and prowl around South St. Paul, where I was born. It's odd driving these streets, remembering some houses, feeling a pull of . . . something. My folks left for California when I was two, my sister Sally about seven and my brother Jim just a baby, so the actual memories are from our annual summer trips back to reconnect with family. But the stories we heard so many times occasionally seem to bring forth vestiges of earlier memories, hints of things seen, faces known, shadows of long, long ago . . .

I'd called my cousin Bob Scheerer and arranged to take him and his wife Sis out to lunch. When I get to his house, I learn that he has called another cousin, Dave Canniff, who drove up from Hastings with his wife Belinda, and yet another cousin, Barry Cosgrove, who stopped by. Bob and Dave are the sons of two of my mom's sisters and Barry, unless I'm mistaken (which is quite possible given the size of this family), is the son of one of her brothers. There are many more, needless to say, but given the craziness of my schedule I didn't want impose on too many of them.

It was nice to check in, though, to laugh, catch up, remember old times and pay tribute to those now gone.

Two interviews in the morning, so an early night, for once.

DAY TWENTY-FOUR

Monday, June 2, 2008

CITY OF ORIGIN: MINNEAPOLIS, MN
MILES TRAVELED: 271

CITY OF DESTINATION: SIOUX FALLS, SD
VENUE: BARNES & NOBLE—SIOUX FALLS

It's all downhill from here—or so it would seem. South and then westward toward home. Mule and I get a late start because of a live radio interview I have to do from the hotel before we take off. And, once we get going, heading south and west out of Minneapolis, the city continues to be just as confusing as has been every other drive here. One-way streets and construction and detours have thrown me off since we got into town Saturday. And I couldn't understand why everything was so screwy until I remembered the bridge collapse last August. Of course! Losing one of the city's main arteries must have created chaos. And trying to reroute everyone who used that bridge has to be madness. So I guess I can be a little more understanding and a lot more patient.

It does piss me off, though, how a study said the money necessary to examine and retrofit the bridges in the U.S. would be less than $20 billion, but we somehow can't afford it—while Bush spends that much in a few weeks in Iraq.

Down to the southern part of the state, almost to Albert Lea before turning west toward South Dakota, it appears everything I said about Iowa applies here too. Flat, slightly sculpted land, well-tended homes, barns, fields and pastures paint a very attractive picture. Add Minnesota to the warm, pleasant, Norman Rockwell heartland feeling I ascribed to Iowa.

They even have the same graceful windmills here. And a town named Blue Earth. What's blue about it isn't immediately evident, but I love the name.

The BBC—which is a breath or fresh air on the radio: actual news—says the UN Food and Security Summit is in an uproar because of world-wide food shortages. It'll take a $60 billion–per-year contribution from the donor nations to see to it that the people of the world have their fundamental nutritional needs met. Yet others are saying there is sufficient soil, seed and ability to provide plenty of food that is not being realized because of subsidies, imposed tariffs, and other methods of economic strangulation used by the U.S. and the European Community that are impacting the underdeveloped world, underselling their own farmers and causing them to go out of business. Fair trade, they say, can solve the problem.

Another source of contention at the conference is the presence of Robert Mugabe, who has ruled Zimbabwe in an increasingly tyrannical manner for nearly thirty years. The irony is that as the leader of the Zimbabwe African National Union (ZANU) who fought and ultimately expelled the racist white Rhodesian regime, he was hailed as a hero in Africa and supported by many freedom-loving Americans, including my friend, the late Allard Lowenstein. A classic example of the corrupting influence of power, the country has suffered increasingly as his leadership descended into antiwhite racism, ruthless, autocratic oppression of his own people and self-serving policies that have destroyed its economy and turned it from a stable, food-exporting country (called by some "the breadbasket of Africa") into a debtor nation now suffering hyper-inflation. People are starving and leaving the country in droves. An opposition political group, struggling to survive where others have been crushed, may have actually succeeded recently in winning power at the ballot box, but are now facing brutal opposition and legal and political chicanery from Mugabe's forces who are trying to change the results.

In the face of all this, Mugabe's arrival at the Food and Security Summit has caused outrage among some of the member nations in attendance, with one British delegate calling his presence "obscene."

I heard Phyllis Bennis, an old friend from the Institute for Policy Studies (IPS), interviewed about the question of Mugabe's attendance and she framed the dilemma nicely, saying that the mandate of the Food and Agriculture Organization (FAO) is to bring nations together to deal with the issue of food security, so it cannot be expected to handle human rights issues outside

---

FROM *THE JOURNEY AND THE GRACE*
by Gary A. Westgard

"August 29, 2006"

Today, in South Dakota,
we plan to kill a man,
the state, all of us, so
students in school
have the opportunity
for discussion, and over
lunch, between bites,
old men can debate
gas prices and lethal
injection and a woman
questioned at the mall
says she wants to
be there to watch, but
a high school student
has homecoming

---

their scope at the same time. When pressed about Mugabe's participation, she said that all countries are invited and the FAO can't tell them who they can or cannot send to represent them. If they were to do that, she pointed out, there could be objections raised to North Korea's being represented by Kim Jong Il because of his human rights violations, or to George W. Bush's presence for the same reason.

Made me laugh.

Food security is a very serious issue, however. UN Secretary General Ban Ki-moon called hunger "the most degrading human condition" and insisted that subsidies and tariffs imposed by the West to support their own farmers must be dealt with.

Flying low into South Dakota, Mule got me to Sioux Falls in time to check into the hotel and do a quick and much-needed load of laundry before changing and heading over to Barnes & Noble for tonight's gig.

Senator George McGovern told me he'd try to be there to introduce me, but I knew it would be hard since the much-touted "last of the primaries" are here and in Montana tomorrow. It was nice of him to say he'd try. When I found out that Hillary, Bill, and Chelsea Clinton were all here in Sioux Falls tonight and

> to plan, so hasn't thought much about this man who will die, who did a terrible thing, who killed another human being, and today we plan to show this man how wrong it is to kill another human being, by killing a human being. Today, in South Dakota the Shepherd will leave the ninety-nine in the wilderness, go off after the one which is lost, and when he has found it, he will lay it on his shoulder and cut its throat.

having a big event at the Fairgrounds, I thought, *Oh shit, it's the Pens again.* Being up against the Penguins in Pittsburgh and the Beer Festival in Minneapolis had been responsible for the only two disappointing turnouts so far, but this promised to be possibly the worst yet.

And boy was I wrong! I got to Barnes & Noble a bit early and there was already a small group gathered, which at least reassured me that it wouldn't be a blowout, but the manager asked me to stand by for a while because, she said, people often showed up at the last minute. And by the appointed time, I was warmly greeted by a hell of a crowd.

I must say it turned out to be one of the best evenings yet. When I thanked them for coming, particularly in view of the competition in town, a woman called out, "We've already made up our minds!" Everybody laughed and it just got better from there. The questions were terrific, ranging all over the map. There was a lot of talk about *M*A*S*H*, of course, but we got into politics, the world situation, the Bush administration, torture, and quite a bit about the death penalty. The manager, a young woman, had told me that she had served on a jury for a death case that had caused a storm of controversy in the state. She said it was one of the toughest things she'd ever done. But, she said, when the parents of the murder victim got on the stand and stated that they had forgiven the perpetrator, it was clear that they didn't want to see their daughter's killer executed.

Once the Q&A was over and the book signings and picture taking began, the line of people waiting kept the questions coming. It took a long time to get through it all and I began to worry about keeping everyone there so late, but they were all very patient, cooperative and in such good moods that it was a delight.

One man introduced himself as a retired Lutheran minister and knocked me out by praising the discussion of the death penalty, saying, "You were ministering tonight." He very sweetly handed me a book in which a passage was marked. When I had a chance to look at it, I saw that he was the author, Pastor Gary Westgard (see sidebar, pages 160–1).

Later, as I was about to leave, one of the B&N staff gave me a note from Susan McGovern, George's daughter. She'd been there the whole time, had come at his request to apologize for his inability to be present. The note said, *He was tied up with responsibilities for the Barack Obama campaign today in Mitchell.* She sat through the whole thing, the staffer said, but didn't want to jump the line and had to go.

Don't people just knock you out sometimes?

Day Twenty-Five

Tuesday, June 3, 2008

City of Origin: Sioux Falls, SD   **City of Destination:** Ogallala, NE

Miles Traveled: 507

Travel Day

Today is a drive day. We have to be in Denver tomorrow night and it's over 700 miles, so we'll drive partway today and the rest tomorrow.

It's overcast again, with rain expected. Mule takes me over to a co-op we learned about and I stock up on munchies before hitting the road.

Heading down through South Dakota, the highway swings back into Iowa (or maybe Iowa sticks into South Dakota) for a while before we cut west toward Nebraska. Rolling hills here, and more cattle than I've seen for a while, but still lots of agriculture—beautiful green fields.

Leaving South Dakota, we pass another town with a great name: Friend, Nebraska. Driving through this state takes me back a number of years. When teenagers, my buddy Pat and I hitchhiked to St. Paul to see a girl I had a terrific crush on—the daughter of a family friend. We did okay until we got into Nebraska, where for some reason we just couldn't get a ride. Finally, a state policeman stopped and told us that this was the area where Charles Starkweather and his girlfriend had gone on a killing spree and nobody was going to be willing to pick up a couple of young hitchhikers, so we'd better get on a bus.

Bus, nothing, we thought, we'd just hop a freight train. And we did, from North Platte to Grand Island. Problem was, it was at night, it was colder than hell, and, unable to find an open boxcar, we hopped onto a flat car. I don't think I've ever been so cold in my life. Pat and I ended up huddled together trying to keep from freezing to death, waiting for the train to slow down enough for us to hop off.

Adventuresome youth . . .

Well, Mule and I just passed the town of Alda, Nebraska. I wonder if he knows . . .

Did I say Iowa was flat? Nebraska is FLAT.

Lots of history here, though. We just passed what they claim is the original Pony Express station. And then Buffalo Bill Cody's Ranch. Rough and ready folks.

Shit. I just learned that Bill Ford passed away. A good man. Bill's sister, Ita Ford, was one of the four North American churchwomen raped and murdered by the Salvadoran military in 1980. He and I were together on a human rights delegation to El Salvador a couple of years later. Bill had become a passionate advocate for human rights and, unwilling to accept that the verdict against the five lower-level National Guardsmen did anything to resolve the issue or punish those truly responsible, he was intent on seeing to it that some of the higher-ups in the Salvadoran military were brought to justice for the murder of his sister and her colleagues. As Bill said, investigating his sister's murder had "radicalized" him. He called the Salvadoran military leadership "a group of gangsters in uniform." And he was ultimately instrumental in getting a $55 million judgment in a U.S. court six years ago against General José Guill-ermo García and General Carlos Eugenio Vides Casanova, two of the worst thugs who ran the military in that country.

On the upside, the news says that Barack Obama has secured enough delegates to clinch the nomination and become the Democratic candi-date for the presidency! It's been a long and complicated journey, so I'll wait to hear more before letting myself celebrate, but if it's official, this is a great day for the U.S.A.

If it's true that Hillary now wants to be his running mate, I hope he doesn't give in. She'd be much better on the Supreme Court.

Too many miles. Time to turn in.

DAY TWENTY-SIX

Wednesday, June 4, 2008

CITY OF ORIGIN: OGALLALA, NE

MILES TRAVELED: 213

CITY OF DESTINATION: DENVER, CO

VENUE: TATTERED COVER BOOK STORE

EVENT COSPONSOR

ACLU of Colorado

A fter spending the night in Ogallala, Nebraska, Mule and I take off and soon cross into Colorado's rolling brown hills with dark clouds gathering before us and storm and tornado warnings being broadcast.

Also being broadcast are the squeals of Rush Limbaugh, whose outrage at the success of Barack Obama is palpable. The list of adjectives he rains on those stupid enough to vote for this upstart is long and demeaning, but it's not quite enough to disguise the abject terror he clearly feels at the possibility of an Obama presidency. It's as though he fears that the change in this country promised by such a development threatens to make him and his ilk a mere asterisk in history. And maybe he's right. At any rate, his tenuous grasp on reality is exemplified this morning by rants against "the Global Warming hoax" and the announcement that the five percent unemployment rate—evidently a right-wing staple—means that "anybody willing to work has a job."

Switching away, I run into the dulcet tones of Dennis Prager, easily the most pompous, self-righteous, and self-satisfied of radio's right-wing blatherers. Prager, too, is clearly terrified, caught mid-rant about how America has turned left. We're all Marxists, you know . . .

Another twist of the dial and I actually find some sense on the air. Ed Schultz is commenting on the political developments, telling us that Obama has invited three people to look at vice presidential possibilities for him—and one of the three is Caroline Kennedy. How great to hear that's she's involved to that degree in the campaign!

For a few minutes, I catch up on the phone with a friend who has been representing Governor George Ryan of Illinois. It's such a tragedy that this good man has been locked up on what seem to me to be bogus charges. A complex case involving assertions of cronyism and abuse of power, it really arose out of a public campaign that falsely blamed him for an accident that killed six children and severely burned their parents. A piece of equipment fell off a truck and struck the family's car, puncturing its gas tank and causing a devastating fire. The truck driver, it turned out, had gotten his license illegally by bribing an employee of a department under Ryan's supervision when he was

ACLU OF COLORADO

The mission of the ACLU of Colorado is to protect, defend, and extend the civil rights and civil liberties of all people in Colorado through litigation, education, and advocacy. We share Mike's passion for human rights, particularly in the areas of criminal justice reform and the abolition of the death penalty. We employ a comprehensive approach to safeguarding freedom—carrying out public education through public forums, events, and position papers, together with our legal work and legislative advocacy. We focus on defending free speech and the right to dissent, securing religious liberty, combating racial and ethnic profiling, and protecting the right to equal treatment for all people, including women, LGBT persons, and immigrants. We have a special concentration on criminal justice reform and ensuring the fair and humane treatment of prison-

secretary of state, before becoming governor. As it turned out, the truck driver was not at fault, Ryan had not hired the dishonest employee who sold the license and had no actual responsibility for the entire event. But the furor from the campaign resulted in an investigation and charges on other issues that, while defensible, fed into an emotional tide that ultimately ruined him. Our hope was that the Supreme Court would overturn the conviction based on the incredibly poor conduct of the trial judge and some craziness with the jury, but that didn't happen; so now they're trying to examine what options are left.

Having known Ryan since he declared a moratorium on the death penalty in Illinois in 2000 after being confronted with a system so shoddy that more people had been freed from his death row than had been executed, I have found him to be a man of character. A self-described "conservative Republican death penalty supporter," Ryan had the personal integrity to recognize a failing system and take the steps necessary to fix it, if possible. Watching the change in him over the years it took to examine the system, and seeing him deal with the political pressure he experienced from every quarter, it was wonderful to see an elected official actually take his job seriously.

ers. Our efforts during Colorado's 2008 legislative session resulted in the passage of a pair of bills concerning the retention of DNA evidence. Coloradans learned firsthand about the importance of DNA evidence this year with the long-overdue release of Tim Masters, who spent nearly a decade in prison for a murder he did not commit. On the death penalty front, we successfully defeated an attempt—one of many across the nation—to use public fear and sentiment to set a terrible legal precedent. SB 195: Death Penalty for Aggravated Sexual Assault on a Child would have, for the first time, mandated the capital punishment for a crime that does not result in the victim's death. Its defeat marked a small victory in the fight against the death penalty—if only by preventing a step backwards. We also work to prevent the abuse of police power through numerous lawsuits addressing excessive force and careless police procedure.

I really grew to like George Ryan for the methodical way he went about the task he set for himself, but when he had the courage and personal integrity to buck the political tide and do what was clearly the right thing in his eyes, he became a hero to me. To have him now in this awful situation is a tragedy. My heart breaks for him and for his wife, Lura Lynn.

Reaching Denver, we find the Oxford Hotel, a grand old place in Lo Do (lower downtown), a revitalized area near the train station. It's a great building just a block away from the Tattered Cover Book Store, where I'm to do a reception for the ACLU of Colorado and then the book event, which they are cosponsoring.

After a late lunch at a good vegetarian restaurant and an invigorating walk through downtown, I change and head to the Tattered Cover, which is in a terrific old three-story brick structure, a refurbished cannery. It's a fabulous place with two extensive floors of books of all types and old, overstuffed chairs and sofas set around so that people can relax and enjoy them.

The folks from the ACLU are terrific and the event goes well. With an introduction by Cathy Hazouri, President of the ACLU of Colorado, the evening's discussion tends to focus more on political and social issues, again with special attention to the death penalty, than on Hollywood and *M*A*S*H*, but that's fine with me. And, of course, *M*A*S*H* always finds a way to fit in.

I'm thrilled that Michael Radelet, Chair of the Department of Sociology at the University of Colorado at Boulder, has come down for the event. Mike has become a valued friend and is one of the great, if unsung, heroes of the death penalty abolition movement. His books, essays, studies, polls, and lectures on the subject provide the basis for some of the most important work done on the issue today. Here in Colorado he has pioneered an effort to bring families still impacted by unsolved murders together with legislators to call for the elimination of the death penalty, with the money wasted on the killing system instead being used to fund efforts to resolve these "cold cases."

Another good night. Back to the Oxford to turn in as the threatened rainstorm finally shows up. No tornadoes, thank you, at least so far. Given all this, though, it may be a long and tricky drive to Park City, Utah tomorrow.

DAY TWENTY-SEVEN

Thursday, June 5, 2008

CITY OF ORIGIN: DENVER, CO

MILES TRAVELED: 517 MILES

CITY OF DESTINATION: PARK CITY, UT

VENUE: PARK CITY LIBRARY

The rain woke me up—a good thing because the hotel's wake-up call never came.

Mule and I head out in a downpour amid radio reports of flooding in some intersections and high water on the highways. The rain is coming down in sheets, but once on the highway the worst part is the wall of water sent up by the semis. If one is in front of us, the wipers can't get the water off the windshield fast enough. When passing, there are moments when it feels as though we're completely submerged. Blind as a bat, I'm forced to read our progress by the proximity to the truck we're passing. Unwilling, or unable, to take my eyes off the windshield in the hope of a momentary view of the road ahead, the side of the semi has to be read by peripheral vision. Gets to be pretty scary a couple of times, but Mule is indomitable.

Mercifully, the rain slows as we move north into Wyoming and then west. And I must say, after going through the Plains states, Wyoming

172

actually begins to feel like it. As we climb to higher altitude, snow still on the hills beside us, the ruptured land looks more and more like the Old West. I don't know if it's the result of seismic activity or the leavings of a passing glacier, but the rugged land boasts oddly shaped rock outcroppings that are weirdly attractive.

Thinking of Wyoming, though, rugged Western beauty is not the first thing that comes to mind. Former Senator Alan Simpson's incredibly snide, unforgivably brutal treatment of Anita Hill during the Senate hearings on Clarence Thomas's nomination to the Supreme Court, a transparent attempt to savage her in order to save his president's hapless nominee, is one thought that occurs. Another is that this is the place that gave us an even more infamous troglodyte—the member of the U.S. Congress who refused to support sanctions on South Africa's apartheid regime, called Nelson Mandela a terrorist, and who later became Secretary of Defense under George H.W. Bush . . . and finally manipulated his way into the vice presidency of the United States so he could rule the world. What is it about the politics of this state?

Pulling off to fill up, I am once again required to pay over $4 per gallon of the cheapest gas—$4.08, to be exact. And, wanting to be sure the last mileage calculation was correct, I check it again. After doing some significant climbing, Mule is still getting forty-one miles per gallon. Better than twice what I get in my pickup at home.

Pulling out, I note that there's suddenly another icon lit up on the dash. This one an exclamation point inside a kind of U. Unsure what it might mean, I assume the exclamation point is saying it's not good, so I pull over and try to figure it out. Sure enough, it's identified in the owner's manual as an alarm. Wonderful, but it doesn't say what kind of alarm. How helpful.

I can sense nothing in the way Mule is behaving to suggest a problem, but I'm not eager to have something fall off or blow up in the middle of a wild and lonely stretch of Wyoming highway. Cheney or Simpson might just happen by and run me over.

I notice that the U the exclamation point sits in has a sort of flat bottom. Could it represent a tire? I get out and look and they all seem fine. Deciding to drive on, I wrestle with the problem. I have to get to Park City, but this damned light won't go away. Figuring this is nuts, I stop again and search the manual one more time. And, finally, I find it! I was right, it means there's something wrong with a tire. Okay, none are flat and we're still able to roll, so on we go. A few miles further down the line there's a sign indicating gas at a place called Elk Station, so I pull off and investigate. It's a pretty forlorn area with one station and not much else. Seeing no sign of an air hose, I step inside and find a friendly woman who directs me to a red hose in the back—if I'll just wait, as she has to switch on the compressor. No problem and thank you, ma'am.

Unsure of the proper pressure, I check each tire and put some air in every one. The last one, the left rear, does seem to be lower than the others, so I even them out and hope this solves the problem. Thanking the friendly woman, I fire up Mule and am disappointed to see that the damned light is still on. Having few options, I put her in gear and pull back onto the highway and Mule, her hoof now apparently comfortable, turns out the light!

Zen and the art of Mule maintenance.

Back on the road the radio says Hillary Clinton has indicated she will "suspend" her campaign. Suspend? That doesn't exactly sound like ending it, does it? There are also reports that two different groups of Hillary supporters are circulating petitions demanding that she be named the vice presidential nominee. Lanny Davis, the lawyer responsible for one of them, says Hillary was told of the effort and didn't endorse it, but didn't tell him to quit. This is not good.

The BBC says Zimbabwe's police have "detained" U.S. and British diplomats who were traveling in the country. Also not good.

Furthermore, Zimbabwe's authorities have "detained" Morgan Tsvangirai, the opposition politician whose campaign threatens to unseat Robert Mugabe. Yet another not good.

And, Zimbabwe has decided to expel all international nongovernmental aid organizations on the pretext that they have been involving themselves in the country's politics and are supporting the opposition. Very not good.

Lots of not good in the news this morning.

Khalid Sheikh Mohammed (KSM, to the intel folks) appeared before a military tribunal at Guantánamo today and reportedly told the presiding judge that the procedure was an "inquisition," that he and his co-defendants had been tortured for years and everyone knew it, and that he wanted to be sentenced to death so that he could be a martyr.

Hmmm. Sort of takes the sting out of the death penalty, doesn't it?

After a lengthy description of the circumstances of the trial and the fact that there are challenges to this process yet to be decided by the Supreme Court, the reporter cites observers from human rights organizations who condemn the entire setup as having been completely tainted by the use of torture to gain confessions.

In fact, an earlier report indicated that while under torture, KSM confessed to things the intelligence people are pretty sure he didn't do, a testament to the value of information forced out through these grisly means.

A lawyer from the Bush administration, however, leapt to the defense of these trials, claiming that all the evidence presented to this court would be from statements "voluntarily given" to interrogators in a "clean environment." None of it, he insisted, would be that which was obtained through the use of torture.

"But," the reporter said, "they have been tortured for years."

"Yes," he admitted, "but the statements being presented in court now were not given under torture, they were given afterward, voluntarily."

It boggles the mind. People who were tortured now give incriminating statements voluntarily? Might one not assume that they did so under the impression that if these "voluntary" statements were not forthcoming they might be taken back to the torture chambers?

I wish the reporter had asked, "If these men were so ready and willing to 'volunteer' these incriminating statements, why did they have to be tortured in the first place?"

Clive Stafford-Smith, an English lawyer who worked here in the U.S. for many years in opposition to the death penalty and is now representing a number of those incarcerated in Guantánamo, is also interviewed. He says that the claims made by the government—that the absence of scars on the accused proves that they were not tortured—are nonsense. He is representing a man who was tortured with a razor blade, he explains, so his client certainly has scars, but most of the methods of torture used do not leave scars—water boarding, for example. They all, he emphasizes, leave mental scars that, while not visible, are nonetheless scars in every sense of the word.

Enough, enough. Radio off.

Results of wind or water erosion are visible here. Some very oddly shaped mounds and spires dot the ground as we pass. One area sports a sloping ridge topped with serrated rocks that looks amazingly like the back of a dinosaur—stegosaurus, to be precise.

Suddenly, we're out of the brown, brush-covered highlands and heading down into a beautiful, deep green valley. It turns out to be a series of such valleys that are quite striking, not something I'd have expected to see in Wyoming. The last of them is kind of schizophrenic: on the right it's an almost mesa-like cliff face sculpted out of red rock, while on the left it's a softly sloping, deep green hill climbing away from the road that looks remarkably like the Irish countryside.

Nearing Park City, we are now passing through Coalville, Utah. Boy, that name takes me back! This trip does trigger some memories. One year, on our annual summer trip to visit family in Minnesota, my dad's old clunker couldn't be trusted to make the trip, so he borrowed my older sister's car—she was out of school and working and had been able to buy a used Ford. Well, better than Dad's or not, it broke down in Coalville, Utah, and we had to spend a couple of days in a motel my folks couldn't afford while the car got fixed—something they also couldn't afford. Rather than watch Mom and Dad worry, my brother Jim and I spent a lot of time outside throwing rocks.

But we always remembered Coalville, Utah.

Park City is a lovely little spot. I'm told it is "a liberal enclave in a very red state." I'm put up in a wonderful, comfortable, and very friendly B&B called the Washington School Inn and have time to get situated before going down to the local TV station for an interview and then to the Park City Library for the book event.

A very nice crowd turns up and we have a terrific exchange. Almost all of the questions are about social issues this time, with just a couple about *M*A*S*H*.

After signing a number of books and posing for a few pictures, I'm taken to dinner at a local restaurant where I get to watch the Lakers lose the first game of the championship series to the Celtics.

Another not good.

Day Twenty-Eight
Friday, June 6, 2008

City of Origin: Park City, UT   **City of Destination:** Sacramento, CA

Miles Traveled: 679

Travel Day

Lovely place, the Washington School Inn. The room was great—Shelley would have adored it. If only . . . The bed was huge and soft, what they call a feather bed, I guess, which would not normally have been my choice. I prefer a firm mattress, but this one folded me in its embrace and I slept.

Very warm, friendly people, a good breakfast—this is the kind of place in which one wants more time. But the road beckons.

The clouds are gone, so as Mule and I pull out we get our first full view of Park City and the surrounding mountains. A phenomenal setting; it's easy to understand why someone would want to get up every morning and take in this vista.

Back on Interstate 80 West we're engulfed in beauty. The mountains are absolutely wonderful. But I'll bet the people who have been here for a long time resent all the development that's going on. Little settlements have sprung up all over the hillsides. They all appear to be tastefully done, but there sure are a lot of them . . .

Suddenly the highway becomes a giant slalom, snaking its way down for miles through a magnificent canyon that eventually brings us to Salt Lake City. Given the beauty of all we've seen this morning, it's easy to understand why Brigham Young felt he had brought his people to the Promised Land.

Seeing the city brings back memories, though, some pleasant, some not. I got to know this area fairly well when my partner and I made a movie just north of here in Ogden almost twenty years ago. It was a great time, we were treated well and the picture was pretty good—one of the first for TNT.

The last visit here wasn't fun. William Andrews was about to be executed and I helped his mother meet with Governor Norman Bangerter to plead for his life. It was an incredibly difficult day, as you might imagine. She was magnificent—human, clear, incredibly strong. He was . . . a politician.

Heading west toward the Great Salt Lake makes me wonder if Brigham and his band had second thoughts after getting a mouthful of that water.

Once past the lake, the highway lays out straight as a stick for miles, a ribbon of black bisecting a huge mass of stark white land flatter than Iowa and Nebraska combined. Encircled by distant mountains, this area—plain, desert, salt flats, alkali, whatever—is so barren and inhospitable that it can barely sustain a kind of sickly scrub grass, and that only at its very edges. Miles and miles of this stuff, with nary a tree nor a rock to hide behind in the event someone wants to take a pee.

Then, just off the highway at what I assume to be near the midpoint, is a large, odd . . . something. Sculpture? It's a squarish post off of which hang a few very large, round objects, one of which seems to have fallen off and broken. A modern, minimalist Christmas tree? Perhaps an artist's rendering of the solar system? Maybe it's a statement to space aliens—or possibly a gift from them? I'm sure there's a point to it . . . I guess.

Sculpted-something behind us, we're back to the huge expanse of white nothingness until a new sighting brings a smile. Maybe twenty feet off the road in this blizzard of white, a romantic named James has placed a little wire sign announcing to passersby that *JAMES LOVES BRITT*, only in place of the word *loves* he's put a heart. "Way to go, James!" I shout.

Mule has no comment.

"Oh, come on, it's sweet."

Silent, he's intent on eating up the miles.

Up ahead, maybe it's all the white, maybe it's the heat, but something plays tricks with the eyes. In the distance, the road looks like it's covered with water. I've seen it before on long drives when it's hot and the road is laid out straight ahead. Alternately, it looks like the highway sinks away and a car or truck way up there appears to be floating.

Nearing the end of this phenomenon, a sign identifies it as the Bonneville Salt Flats. Of course, of course, the place where they do all the car commercials or sometimes compete to break the land speed record.

Crossing into the Nevada desert, a dry, mountainous expanse so different from what we've just been through that it's visually interesting . . . for a while. Then I turn on the radio and am lucky enough to find the BBC again.

I catch the end of something indicating that an Israeli official threatened an attack on Iran's nuclear project. I hope they can keep a leash on the hawks over there, because that would be a catastrophe—for Israel, for the entire Middle East, for the world. And, though I only get part of it, this statement seems somehow to be tied to a huge bump in the price of oil today. Ugh.

Things seem to be worsening in Zimbabwe, as well. It sounds as though Mugabe's forces are so intent on maintaining power and so fearful that the election will spell the end of their dominion that they've given up any pretense of honorable behavior. What they're doing describes the collapse of any semblance of justice in that poor country.

Shirin Ebadi, the Iranian human rights activist who was awarded the Nobel Peace Prize in 2003, is interviewed. We met when Human Rights Watch honored her in Los Angeles a year or two before she was awarded the Nobel. Some people are so damned brave it's amazing. Asked about the human rights situation in Iran today, she says it's worse now than eight years ago, but better than twenty-eight years back.

When asked by the BBC interviewer how she keeps from losing hope, she says, "I don't have the right to lose my hope. If I lost hope I could not do my work."

Representative Keith Ellison, Democrat of Minnesota, hosted a community forum on Iran toward the end of May. Iran scholars spoke and answered questions. All three said the Bush administration's approach to Iran is counterproductive, only further entrenching the hardliners at the same time as it makes them more popular among the Iranian people. These men cited the Iranian overture to the U.S., made through the Swiss Embassy in 2003, offering to discuss all the issues of contention between the two countries—including the question of nuclear power—that was brushed off by Bush and Cheney.

Those two are nuts.

And their friends in the U.S. Senate today kept the Global Warming bill from coming to the floor. Nuts, I tell ya.

There was a .5 percent rise in the unemployment rate announced today. Rush will have to alter his rant. And Robert Reich, Secretary of Labor under Clinton, says there is no question but that we are in a recession. (In that regard, a guy I met in Park City last night after the presentation is visiting from Germany. He laughs when he hears Americans scream about paying $4 per gallon for gas. In Germany they're now paying $9.)

The skies are clear out here, but the wind is scary. Every once in a while a huge gust surprises us and threatens to push Mule off the road. It seems to want to happen just when I'm paying attention to some of the interesting rock formations out here. The way the wind—and probably the water—has sculpted some of these rock faces and pillars is glorious. But okay, Mule, I'll keep at least one eye on the road.

Heading into Winnemucca, Nevada makes me laugh. An old pal of mine always wanted to visit, saying it was the only place in America where prostitution is legal. I'm not sure if that's true, but if so it makes me wonder if there will be billboards on the highway advertising the trade. I see none as we come into town, but a sign for a motel offers free movies. Some enterprising pimp should put up one right behind it, saying, *Come to the Chicken Ranch; Make Your Own Movies.*

And then, lo and behold, on the road as we're leaving town there's a sign for the World Famous Mustang Ranch, with a sketch of a woman's face and a phone number. So maybe it is true.

Jesus.

There are lots of cone-shaped hills in the valley here, making me think this must have been a very active volcano site in some long-ago era. The ground is strewn with rocks that might very well have once been lava.

As we approach the Truckee River, the green belt it creates is so vivid it's almost a shock after all the brown we've been through for so many hours. Following the Truckee down through a canyon it has cut through some mountains that look as though they've been wrestled out of the earth, we find ourselves in Reno, Nevada.

I had assumed we'd stop for the night here because Sacramento, where tomorrow's event will be held, looked to be too far for one day's drive—700 miles. But it's still early, the sun is up and we've gained an hour by crossing into the Pacific time zone, so California beckons.

Once past Reno, we're back with the Truckee, following it through another canyon. This one covered with pine trees, a lovely sight after all that dry sand and scrub brush. Climbing through the Sierras is a delight, then we're onto another slalom run down thousands of feet to the valley on the other side. Before my body clock can make any sense of it, we're heading into Sacramento for the night.

A little oops here. We hunt up the bookstore for tomorrow, a Barnes & Noble, and then look for a convenient, nearby motel. Doubletree Inn, full. Red Lion, full. Marriott, full. Best Western, full. What the hell is going on in Sacramento this weekend? We finally find a spot, not so nearby and not so convenient, but Mule is happy, so I am too.

Day Twenty-Nine

Saturday, June 7, 2008

City: Sacramento, CA
Venue: Barnes & Noble—Arden Fair

Event Cosponsor

Death Penalty Focus

I wake up before the alarm this morning with something troubling me. I realize it has been tugging at my subconscious and needs to be dealt with. The Barnes & Noble gig is at noon—they want me to be there by 11:30—so I have time to think about it. And I do.

I get ready, check out and go down to fire up Mule. As always, he starts so quietly the only way I can tell he's running is that the dash lights come on. So I just sit there for a while, waiting. That's unusual, so after a bit I figure he is aware something's up.

"I need to talk to you."

More silence, but I sense a slight up-tick in attention. If he had ears, they'd be pricked up.

"Yesterday, when we were racing through the Great Salt Lake Desert . . ."

There's a slight, almost imperceptible shiver.

"... and I got excited about that *James Loves Britt* sign?"

There it is again.

"It's just that I thought it was sweet and you didn't, uh ... well, it seemed like you didn't kind of 'get it,' you know?"

Now it's clearly a shiver, maybe a quiver.

"Anyway, I've been thinking, and I realize I sort of teased you about it ..."

Snort. Cough.

"And, I just ... well, I wasn't thinking. That was out of line. So I just wanted to say I'm sorry."

Cough. Quiver. Snort!

"Look, pal ... just take it easy. I don't mean for this to be uncomfortable. All I'm trying to say is that in thinking about it, I realized that you ... you don't ... Foofff ... Look, what I'm trying to say is, you, uh, you're a ... you're a ... a hybrid. Right?"

Ssssssigggggghhhhh.

"Right. So ... you don't ... I mean ... you're not ... there's no, uh ... It kinda doesn't happen for you, huh?"

"Uh-uh."

"Yeah. Yeah, I get that. I mean, it just came to me, but ... I guess I hadn't thought about it, because ... well, you know. We've been together ... and you seem perfectly ... you know."

Quiver.

"And, uh ... so, uh ... emotional ... stuff. There's none of that with your kind, right?"

"Uh-uh."

"Yeah. No, I get that. I get that. I mean, we are what we are, right?"

"Uh-huh."

"Right."

We sit there for a while.

"Okay. Well, I just wanted to be sure you understood that I didn't mean to make you uncomfortable."

"Uh-huh."

"And that I'm sorry if I did."

"Uh-huh."

"Okay. So, we're all right?"

"Uh-huh."

"Good. So, I guess it's time to go."

"Yes."

"Okay." I reach for the little funky plastic knob on a short stick to put it in reverse, but I stop. "But you kind of like me, huh?"

BIG quiver. Shake, snort!

"Okay, okay, whoa. Whoa! Don't have a breakdown. Easy now! Easy, pal, easy! It's okay. No problem. Not another word. We're going." I put the little funky plastic knob on a short stick into reverse, back out, put it into drive and we head down the street.

"But you do. I know you do."

Mule bucks, the tires squeal and we're off. But unless I'm imagining it, the dash lights shine just a bit brighter.

Barnes & Noble is in a big shopping mall called the Arden Fair and I find a spot for Mule under a tree—it's getting hot—and go in. I'm a bit early, so there's time to nose around while things get set up. Suddenly, Ellen Eggers comes up and gives me a hug. A public defender here in Sacramento, Ellen is also on the board of Death Penalty Focus. One of the most positive, energetic, kind and thoughtful people I've ever met, she's always smiling, always working, offering, volunteering, finding ways to be helpful. Given the milieu in which she works, protecting the rights of people charged with—often convicted of, guilty or not—quite grievous crimes, her deep well of sweetness is astonishing. Today, typically, she made up flyers about my appearance here and has been handing them out along with literature about our organization (I work with her at DPF). And right behind Ellen is Greg Wilhoit—simply stated, a hero. Greg was tried, convicted, and sentenced to death in Oklahoma for murdering his wife. He served six years on Oklahoma's death row before a courageous attorney exposed the shoddy work of the prosecutor, proved Greg innocent of the crime and got him set free. Rather than turning into an angry, bitter man raging at what a crooked prosecutor, junk science and the state of Oklahoma did to him, Greg volunteers his time working with organizations like ours. He talks to schools, churches and any group that will hear him about fixing the

DEATH PENALTY FOCUS

Mike Farrell has been the president of Death Penalty Focus (DPF) for more than fifteen years. Founded in 1988, DPF is one of the largest nonprofit advocacy organizations in the nation dedicated to the abolition of capital punishment through public education, grassroots and political organizing, research, media outreach, local, national, and international coalition building, and the education of religious, legislative, and civic leaders about the death penalty and its alternatives. DPF has eleven active volunteer chapters in California and more than 25,000 members and supporters worldwide.

We believe that the death penalty is an ineffective, cruel, and simplistic response to the serious and complex problem of violent crime. It institutionalizes discrimination against the poor and people of color, diverts attention and financial resources away from preventative measures that would actually increase public safety, risks the execution of innocent people, and does not deter crime.

DPF sponsors research projects and opinion polls, organizes year-round public education and professional media campaigns, and conducts major conferences, seminars, and workshops. We produce and distribute a variety of publications and manage a top-ranked interactive website. DPF has also de-

chaos and corruption in the criminal justice system and the need to eliminate this awful, dehumanizing process of state killing that almost cost him and 128 other wrongly convicted people their lives.

Soon a nice group is gathered and again we have a good time.

veloped an educational curriculum for high school teachers interested in discussing the death penalty with their students. We also mobilize death penalty opposition by organizing educational events, rallies, vigils, and other public demonstrations.

Current DPF projects include the following: California Crime Victims for Alternatives to the Death Penalty seeks to identify, organize, and empower the families, friends, and loved ones of murder victims who oppose the death penalty; Law Enforcement Outreach Project recruits and mobilizes law enforcement and seeks to increase their visibility as opponents of the death penalty; Clergy Mobilization Project seeks to organize the faith community against the death penalty; Faces of Wrongful Conviction Project brings the voices of men and women who were wrongfully convicted, including former prosecutors, judges, and legal experts who oppose the death penalty, to the public's awareness; Unrepresented Death Row Prisoner Project provides unrepresented, indigent prisoners on California's death row with access to basic living supplies; Californians for a Moratorium on Executions is an ongoing campaign to initiate a moratorium on executions; the International Outreach and Communications Project (IOCP) is dedicated to facilitating the development of collaborative strategies and supportive relationships between U.S. and European Union advocates for alternatives to the death penalty.

These talks—particularly the Q&A sessions—are a lot of fun. I don't know if I ever do it quite the same way twice, except for one story I love to tell, but the people who come are always thoughtful, interested, considerate, and appreciative. Periodically I'm challenged about something, the death penalty, for example, but that only provides more opportunity to explain why it's so wrong.

One more under my belt, I unhitch Mule and we head to San Francisco, which will be our base for the next few days. This will give Mule some time to catch his breath and me the chance to do another load of laundry.

From the news, I learn that Hillary has endorsed Obama, beginning the healing process necessary for the Democrats to put together a winning strategy for November.

Though I don't like the fact that she continues to use the word "suspend" in reference to her own campaign, I'm glad for the endorsement.

I'm not happy to learn that Senator Obama, in speaking to the American Israel Public Affairs Committee (AIPAC), has apparently voiced his support for making Jerusalem the "undivided" capital of Israel. That's just a sop to the Israeli right-wing. Resolving the status of Jerusalem should be left to the negotiations that need to be held between Israelis and Palestinians to establish two sovereign and independent states, living side by side, with guarantees of peace and security for both. Within those negotiations a satisfactory solution can, I believe, be found to deal with the desire of both of these peoples to have their capital in Jerusalem. One way to achieve that, of course, is to establish Jerusalem as an international city and provide an area for the capital of each country within its boundaries. But it serves no productive purpose at this juncture for a U.S. leader to make a declaration on Jerusalem's future in favor of one state as opposed to the other. All that does is underscore the U.S. bias in favor of Israel that so angers the Arab world.

Once set up at the Rex Hotel in San Francisco, I get to have dinner with Robyn Hernandez, an old friend and another Death Penalty Focus board member. I've known Robyn since she was in school. To see her now as a mom and a high school teacher is a trip.

It'll be nice to have a bit of time in the city since I'm usually here only for board meetings and then on the first plane home. But I sure wish Shelley was here with me. Me and Mule, I mean . . .

Day Thirty
Sunday, June 8, 2008

City of Origin: San Francisco, CA **City of Destination:** Corte Madera, CA

Miles Traveled: 15 **Venue:** Book Passage

Event Cosponsor
Death Penalty Focus

U p early again, but not so far to drive this day. Henry Tennenbaum's show is live on KRON-TV bright and early on Sunday morning here in San Francisco, so I'm happy to stop in. And it's an extra pleasure this morning, as the guest preceding me is Will Durst, a very bright and extraordinarily funny guy who satirizes political figures on both sides of the aisle. Will and I first met when he appeared at a benefit for Artists United to Win Without War, the group Robert Greenwald and I started in the hope of raising the level of debate in the country and awakening the American people before Cheney/Bush invaded Iraq. (We failed.) Will really makes me laugh. To my delight, he has helped us by appearing at DPF's "Stand Up for Justice" comedy night a number of times since.

Henry is fun and very energetic, so he fits a lot of information into a short interview and then I'm out of there in time for Mule and me to make our way to the North Beach area and another interview, this with Brian Copeland on KGO radio's *Newstalk*. Brian is another stand-up comic who has appeared for us on DPF's comedy night. He's also a very astute commentator and a talented writer. His book, *Not a Genuine Black Man,* is at once a funny and tragic tale of his young life and a searing indictment of the racial bias in San Leandro, California, not too many years ago.

Interviews out of the way, our next stop is at Book Passage in Corte Madera, California, about ten minutes north of the Golden Gate Bridge. Elaine Petrocelli, the proprietor, is a passionate champion of books, a respected community leader, and a fierce defender of the endangered independent bookstore. She, her husband, and their events manager, Kate Ferguson, provide their devoted customers the opportunity to meet many of the significant authors who pass through the Bay Area and they were even able to slip me into the mix.

This is actually my second time at Book Passage—Shelley and I were here when the book came out in hardcover over a year ago—and the enthusiastic embrace offered today makes it feel a lot like coming home.

The event is cosponsored by Death Penalty Focus and my friends Lance Lindsey and Stefanie Faucher, respectively the Executive Director and Program Director of DPF, are there to provide support, answer questions about our work and offer opportunities for people to become involved. These two are truly the dynamic duo of DPF. Lance is that wonder of wonders, a blindingly intelligent, soft-spoken, dedicated, kind, graceful, and completely self-effacing man who does this work because his principles demand it. He's become a true and trusted friend. Stefanie, far too young to have the grasp of issues and organizational genius she demonstrates daily, simply astounds us all with her energy and commitment. Along with another ally, Natasha Minsker of the ACLU of Northern California, Stefanie was named Abolitionist of the Year by the National Coalition to Abolish the Death Penalty. When we end this blight, she will have been one of the primary reasons why.

A large and enthusiastic group has gathered and Elaine, already a regular and generous supporter, introduces me and kindly announces that ten percent of any sales during this afternoon's event will be donated to DPF. The presentation itself seems to go well and, in short, we have a ball—might even have recruited some new members.

In the evening, DPF board member Elizabeth Zitrin and her husband Clint host Stefanie, Lance, his wife Ruta and me for dinner at Ristorante Milano, a wonderful little Italian place on Russian Hill in which they share part ownership. Elizabeth, an attorney and a fountain of energy, serves not only on our board but is also Death Penalty Abolition Coordinator for Amnesty International, on the board of the ACLU of Northern California, on the advisory board for the Northern California Innocence Project, and represents DPF on the steering committee of the World Coalition Against the Death Penalty in Europe, where she chairs the USA Working Group. As said, a fountain of energy.

After a wonderful meal, Mule ushers me gently through the streets of San Francisco and back to the Rex Hotel.

Day Thirty-One

Monday, June 9, 2008

City of Origin: San Francisco, CA

Miles Traveled: 15

City of Destination: Oakland, CA

Venue: Barnes & Noble—Jack London Square

Event Cosponsor

Death Penalty Focus

I t's an odd sensation to wake up in the same city I woke up in yesterday without someplace to rush off to. So I decided to check something out.

One of the people who came to the event at Book Passage yesterday was Nan Sincero, who is on the staff of Centerforce, a San Rafael–based nongovernmental organization that provides support, education and advocacy "for individuals, families and communities impacted by incarceration." In other words, they offer help, education and direction for prisoners, ex-prisoners and family members of both. You know, the kind of assistance you'd think the government of a civilized country would provide its citizens.

Centerforce works to bridge the yawning gap between the society that punishes people by shutting them away in "animal factories" and forgets about them, and the society that expects them to behave like thoughtful, productive citizens when they come out.

The dissonance makes me think of Ernie, a tough former drug addict I once knew who worked with people who were trying to get their lives together. Someone used the word "rehabilitation" in reference to the work he was doing, and Ernie said, "Rehabilitation, bullshit! These people have never been habilitated in the first place."

Like Ernie, Centerforce understands that too many in our society haven't had either the education or the life experience needed to provide them with the tools—and the self-esteem—necessary to build a productive life. When they run afoul of the law and end up in the system, they're seen as "wrongdoers"; they become things—not people—that need to be punished and controlled. Instead of human beings without hope, in need of education and habilitation, they're miscreants to be handled, usually in ways that are demeaning and dehumanizing. And when released they're thus likely to be more lost, angry and antisocial than when they went inside. But thinking of them as humans in need of attention doesn't play well with the "tough-on-crime" crowd, so politicians preen and growl and spend our money building more and bigger prisons rather than providing the programs that will actually help people straighten out their lives.

Politicians having failed, Centerforce has picked up the fallen flag. And Nan Sincero, who works with them, stopped in to say hello and pass on some information. We had met earlier this year when I spoke at a conference she organized, and she presented me afterward with a beautiful wooden box that had been made by a convict in San Quentin. It is truly a work of art, carefully crafted and delicately detailed, and shows extraordinary talent on the part of its creator, a man named Brad Benito, who has developed what is clearly a valuable skill in the prison workshop.

Touched by the gift and thrilled at its beauty, I told her at the time that I'd like to go up to the San Quentin gift shop when next in the area to see about buying some more boxes. They'd make wonderful presents and their purchase would mean some money—and perhaps, most importantly, some attention and appreciation—for the artist who did such fine work.

Her purpose in seeking me out at last night's event, Nan said, was to let me know that if I did want to go up to the gift shop, I'd better hurry. They're shutting down the program. At first I couldn't believe my ears. They're shutting down a program that offers inmates the chance to learn a craft, to develop a skill, to begin to believe they're capable of doing something worthwhile? Why?

She'd asked the warden, she said, and was first told it was a matter of money, then that it was a lack of teachers, and finally that it was simply a directive from the top of the Department of Corrections and there was nothing he could do about it.

What it is, of course, is a crime. Not the kind one goes to jail for, but rather the kind those with power inflict on those without it, especially the ones about whom no one cares.

So this morning I drive up to San Quentin to buy some more of these creations by the talented men who make them before the program is ended. But when I get there I find the prison gift shop closed. Despite the sign on the door saying that this is the time for it to be open, it's closed. And the guard at the gate has no information about why it is closed and when it might be open.

Standing there at the east gate of this awful place, where I've stood too many times protesting the killing of one of its inmates, it is exactly as I described it in *Just Call Me Mike*: "San Quentin, a dreary leaden lump, sits like a turd on the north shore of picturesque San Francisco Bay. Standing with your back to this house of misery allows in the un-alloyed beauty of the bay, but to turn and face it brings back with a cold slap the depressing reality of our failed system."

Mule carries me quietly back to the city, neither of us having much to say.

In the evening we go over to the Barnes & Noble on Jack London Square in Oakland for another event. Barbara, the events manager, says that from reading my book she is sure I'll appreciate one she re-cently published and gives me a copy. It's a collection of poems written by middle school kids in Oakland, a heartbreaking series of cries from young people yearning for a chance, some attention, a reason to hope. It's wonderful that someone listened and printed their cries, and inspir-ing that these kids were willing to so bare their souls, yet I can't help but wonder how many of them, if not heard, will end up where I stood, so frustrated, earlier today.

A nice group shows up for the book event and most of tonight's discus-sion, interestingly, is about social justice issues, particularly the death penalty. Two people in the group, while not unpleasant about it, just felt strongly that some people don't deserve to live. I explain that I'm not suggesting that my morality is higher than theirs—they have every right to believe as they do—but at a minimum, it seems to me, if you give the state the right to kill, it becomes your responsibility to see to it that the system used is just, fair and incapable of error—of mistakenly killing an innocent person. A rational look at our system exposes it as unjust, unfair, corrupt, and wracked with error. So before the killing begins, one supporting the right to kill has the responsibility to fix the defects that have created a racist system that is only used against the poor, is bankrupting state budgets and encouraging base behavior on the part of police and prosecutors. Once those things are sorted out, the only remaining questions become, *Are we helping or harming our society by stooping to the level of the least among us at his or her worst moment?* and its corollary, *Do we deserve to kill?*

Brian Copeland, the radio talk show host who interviewed me yesterday, comes by as promised, and after the talk we go out to dinner. A very nice man, a new friend.

Day Thirty-Two

Tuesday, June 10, 2008

City: San Francisco, CA
Venue: The Booksmith

Event Cosponsors
Death Penalty Focus, Human Rights Watch

U p and out this morning for an interview on KCBS radio down on Battery Street. Nice couple, Stan and Holly; they cover all the high points and it's quickly over. As Stan said, "In news-talk radio nothing gets more than five minutes and then we're onto the next subject." He is very sweet, though, and when I'm leaving, he gets up, shakes my hand, and says, "Keep on with the good work you're doing."

These little grace notes mean a lot.

I had taken a cab down to the station because I'd been warned that parking might be hard to come by, so since it is a lovely morning and I have nothing on the schedule until the event at The Booksmith later that evening, I decide to walk for a while.

Ambling up the street with nowhere I have to be provides a rare moment of freedom, taking me to a fantasy about a trip on my motorcycle, going "where the front wheel takes you," as another rider once said to me while we boarded a ferry from England to Norway. What an incredible feeling that is.

I'm brought back to the present by the ringing of my cell phone. I keep it on in case Shelley needs to reach me, but it rings so seldomly it's always a surprise. This particular surprise is my friend Blair, from Las Cruces. After I missed seeing him back on Day Four and we caught up by phone, he's taken to checking this tour diary once in a while and dropping me a line via e-mail. Blair and I have known each other since high school and our recent communications have centered on learning that another friend from the old days is quite ill. It's an odd thing to take in, this realization that the circle of friends you've known since childhood has reached the age where disease and too often death is the subject that puts you back in touch. Fortunately for me, this awareness has caused some of our old gang to be more respectful of the passage of time and more inclined to reach out once in a while just to check in, make sure things are okay, and let each other know

HUMAN RIGHTS WATCH

Human Rights Watch is one of the world's leading independent organizations dedicated to defending and protecting human rights. By focusing international attention where human rights are violated, Human Rights Watch gives voice to the oppressed and holds oppressors accountable for their crimes. Human Rights Watch's rigorous, objective investigations and strategic, targeted advocacy build intense pressure for action and raise the cost of human rights abuse. For thirty years, we have worked tenaciously to lay the legal and moral groundwork for deep-rooted change and have fought to bring greater justice and security to people around the world.

Human Rights Watch has offices in many countries and investigates and exposes human rights violations in more than eighty of them. Each year, our staff members conduct more than a hundred fact-finding investigations on pressing abuses and then issue reports to publicize their findings. Human Rights Watch shares its reports with journalists, who often publish the reports' revelations in local and international media. This publicity embarrasses abusive governments in the eyes of their citizens and the world, and spurs leaders to bring abuses to an end. Human Rights Watch meets with government officials, the United Nations, the Euro-

we care. I'm deeply touched, then, when after a brief and, with Blair, always funny conversation, he signs off by saying, "Love you, Mike," words I'm happy to return. And then I continue my stroll through the warm San Francisco morning, a very rich man.

pean Union, the African Union, the Association of Southeast Asian Nations, and other influential actors to advance humane policies and increase pressure for positive change.

In 1997, Human Rights Watch shared the Nobel Peace Prize with its partners in the International Campaign to Ban Landmines, which fought for the creation of the Mine Ban Treaty, now signed by 156 countries. Human Rights Watch is now working on a similar campaign to end the use of cluster munitions. In May 2008, more than 100 countries adopted a treaty banning these indiscriminate weapons. Human Rights Watch created an international coalition to ban the use of child soldiers; after six years of negotiations, governments adopted a treaty prohibiting the use of children as combatants.

Human Rights Watch has blazed a path for international justice, pressing the United Nations to establish the International Criminal Court; calling for the creation of the international war crimes tribunal in Yugoslavia and working with prosecutors to get Slobodan Milosevic indicted; providing expert testimony to the international war crimes tribunal set up to try those responsible for the genocide in Rwanda; and documenting abuses in Sierra Leone's bloody civil war, which helped lead to the creation of the war crimes tribunal that is trying Charles Taylor and other alleged war criminals.

A nonpartisan organization, we do not accept funding from any government.

Once past the strip clubs and topless bars, walking through Chinatown is interesting. If you stop for a minute, watch and listen to the passersby, breathe in the odors and let your eyes move slowly over the signs all around, you can easily be transported far, far away. This is quite a country we live in.

Turning on Powell, I head up to the Fairmont Hotel, wondering if the cable cars are running this early. They are, I learn, so I wait at the corner of Powell and California, in front of the Fairmont, for a ride down memory lane. This is the corner where, as we were leaving a CBS function twenty-six years ago, I asked Shelley—who I really didn't know very well but somehow knew

I didn't want to let escape—if she'd like to take a cable car ride. After a brief hesitation, she said yes.

Long story—much too long to go into here—but, trust me, it's a good one. And the cable car ride in her honor is just right. For some reason, as I'm getting off, the conductor won't take my money, saying, "Free ride today." Maybe he knows.

Back at the Hotel Rex I decide to try the San Quentin Hobby Shop once more. But rather than just drive out there cold again, I try calling to see if I can find out if it will be open. I don't know if you'll ever have occasion to call San Quentin, but if you do you'll find it's a pain in the ass. Everything is robot voices and answering machines. One could easily come to the conclusion that there are no human beings at work there. Well . . . I didn't mean it that way.

Anyway, nothing. Finally, I try Nan Sincero at Centerforce, who apparently knows all the secret combinations. She finds out that the shop is closed again today, though no one seems to know why, except for the possibility that there's been a lockdown at the prison. She'll call me tomorrow morning if she finds out it's open. I have to head out of town tomorrow, but maybe . . .

The Booksmith is out in The Haight, as it's known—or Haight-Ashbury when it was the center of the hippie movement in the '60s. Another independent bookstore trying to survive under the onslaught of the big chains, it's a great place with a wonderful selection. When I arrive, Thomas, the manager, takes me into the back room and asks me to wait awhile even though a number of people are already there, ready for me. Parking is tough here, he says, and—of course—this is The Haight, so he likes to delay the presentations just a bit.

When he comes back to get me it appears he was right, the crowd has swelled considerably. Thomas's introduction is quite complimentary, the kind that's hard to listen to because you're standing right behind him with your face hanging out and it's so embarrassing you want to crawl into a hole somewhere. But he is gracious about it and the crowd is generous in response, so we start on a high note and it seems to sustain.

The areas of interest expressed and the questions asked are "a great mix," as Thomas puts it later, and the time passes swiftly. In trying to bring it to a conclusion, I say, "I don't want to keep you here all night," and one woman calls out, "Oh, we don't mind."

It was that kind of a night. The book signing and picture taking goes well too, with a very enthusiastic young woman from Tennessee topping things off by presenting me with a large, knitted something—I could see this girl and her friend busily working away at it during the entire session, needles flying. It's big, whether a "throw" or a "lap robe" or a knitted poster, I don't really know, but as she unfolds it, the message comes clear: it says *MASH* in yellow letters on a green background. And it's not quite done—hence the furious knitting during the presentation—so she says she'll have to mail it to me. It's all a bit nuts, but she's so charged about it that there's nothing to do but laugh and say thanks.

Back at the Rex, a call to Shelley tells me the Lakers won, which is very good. The Celtics are beginning to scare me.

To bed.

DAY THIRTY-THREE

Wednesday, June 11, 2008

CITY OF ORIGIN: SAN FRANCISCO, CA   **CITY OF DESTINATION:** LOS ANGELES, CA

MILES TRAVELED: 382, VIA SALINAS   **VENUE:** JOHN STEINBECK MUSEUM (SALINAS, CA)

EVENT SPONSOR

John Steinbeck Rotary Club

T he phone wakes me in the morning. It's Nan Sincero from Centerforce, saying the Hobby Shop at San Quentin is open. There's no telling when it might close, she says, but if I want to get in, now is the time.

Scheduled to speak in Salinas tonight, I throw everything together, check out of the hotel and head up across the Golden Gate Bridge hoping we'll luck out this time.

Pulling up, I see a man standing in the doorway of the Hobby Shop, a good sign, so I quickly steer Mule down to the visitor parking area and am frustrated to find it full. Driving back up, I turn toward the gate, hoping to get a chance to ask the guard what to do. He's on a walkie-talkie and has two people standing in front of him, so we stop in the road. He quickly yells, "Get out of the road, you're blocking the gate!"

This is a very small space, so as I jockey Mule around I try to figure out what our options are. The road from the highway up here to the East

Gate is less than a mile long, quite narrow and lined with old wooden houses—this comprising the small community of San Quentin. Most of it is restricted parking. I'd always assumed that the people living here work at or are somehow associated with the prison and therefore not sympathetic to us, but a few years ago a woman opened her door and offered tea and support on a bitter cold night when we were demonstrating against an execution. A nurse who lives in a small apartment behind a large house a ways down the street, she has extended the same warmth and hospitality to our group ever since—I have a picture of a couple of us huddled together with Joan Baez and Jesse Jackson in her small kitchen, probably on the horrible night they killed Stanley Tookie Williams.

But her place is halfway back to the highway, and even if she's home it's probably unlikely there's enough room to park down there. And if I try, that'll probably be when they decide to close the Hobby Shop. Here, though, the area is clearly marked in angry red stripes that indicate there's no parking allowed except for a few spots, probably for employee cars, and they're full.

"To hell with it," I say to Mule, pulling him into the red *No Parking* space in front of the Hobby Shop, "the worst thing that can happen is he yells at me again."

"You hope," Mule whispers encouragingly as I climb out.

Now off the walkie-talkie, the guard is passing the two men through the gate as I approach. "Sorry about blocking the road," I offer, "but the visitor parking area is full and I just wanted to see if there is anywhere else to park so I can get a couple of things at the Hobby Shop."

He looks at me for a moment, then says, "Full, huh?"

"Yeah."

He looks a bit longer, and I'm preparing to hear, *Tough shit*, when he says, "Tell you what. Pull it over there next to the Mustang. Not in the blue area, on the other side."

"Thanks. Thanks very much." And I do.

Inside the small shop the walls are decorated with artwork, most of it pencil sketches, some quite good. Native Americans and black women predominate, though there are some very nicely detailed nature scenes. Old-fashioned display cases are filled with rings, earrings, bracelets and more artwork, a lot of it cartoon-style drawings. I can only find one box of the size I was given by Centerforce, and it's decorated with a carved bird and flower that's a bit too ornate for anyone I can think of. There are a number of smaller boxes, though, that display the same careful artistry and attention to detail as the one I was given. There are also a number of nicely made cable car replicas, some of them mounted, one or two set up as lamps, others as music boxes—and yes, they play "I Left My Heart in San Francisco."

The young man in charge is a nice-looking African American in a loose-fitting red prison jumpsuit, the name *O'Connor* printed on the left side. He's very friendly, has a nice smile and seems eager to help. It turns out he's very excited because he's being released on Saturday. He's got a job waiting for him outside and he's "going to stay straight."

Mr. O'Connor is very meticulous about the paperwork as I buy a few things—if you're about to rush out there, they take no credit cards or checks, only cash—and he explains that about ninety percent of the price paid goes to the artist (which is more than what I'd heard—I hope he has it right).

Wishing him the best, I walk out with my box of gifts and go over to thank the guard. He turns to me and says, "Sorry I yelled at you."

"Not a problem," I reply, surprised.

"My dad was in Korea and he loved your show. Thank you."

As we make our way down that narrow street toward the Richmond Bridge and the road south to Salinas, I shake my head, saying, "Man, you just never know . . ."

"*Man?* You talking to me?"

"Sorry. It's just an expression."

"For some."

"Uh-huh. Well . . . Huh. Lots of things to think about."

Words have weight, so it's worth being careful about their use. And, in thinking about the guard, one just never knows—about people, either.

Salinas is a couple of hours down Highway 101 and thus closer to home, which is good, but I'm a little unclear as to what's expected of me when I get there. Mark Kimber, another friend from the Death Penalty Focus board, has been asking for months if I'd be willing to come speak to his Rotary Club, and this, since I'd be going right through there, seemed the logical time. (Who knew I'd be exhausted and brain-dead from this five-week, 8,000-plus mile marathon?)

Mark is a good guy (he bristles if I say sweet), a small-business owner in a heavily agriculture-dependent area and a Rotarian. He continues to insist he's more conservative than most of us on the board, while being one of our most reliable and dependable volunteers at any and every event. Small speaking engagement, large fundraiser or in between, Mark and Phyllis, his terrific wife, are there taking tickets, passing out literature, pouring drinks, moving furniture, or whatever else is needed. And they're always there for the clean-up detail. Generous to a fault and committed to eliminating state killing, he acts as the secretary at our board meetings and regularly spices things up with his wry and irreverent sense of humor. And, go figure, he's a vegetarian and an expert skydiver.

Parking Mule, I walk into his travel agency and am quickly taken out to lunch at a local health food place he's found. I again try to pin him down on what these folks expect to hear from me, and he remains vague, saying that since they haven't arranged to have a supply of books to sell I can talk about anything I want. They are a pretty conservative bunch, he says, but they'll be open to whatever I want to say. He has, he thinks, amply covered the subject of the death penalty with them through other guests he's brought in, but it's been awhile, so . . .

Mark has booked a hotel room for me, but when he says the meeting starts at 6 and will probably be over by 8:30, I ask him to cancel it so I can try driving home tonight. That worries him; it's another 350 miles. But if I wear out, I assure him, I can get a room down the road somewhere. It just seems crazy to be this close to home and not get there.

He has business to take care of and we have a couple of hours before the meeting, so I walk up to the John Steinbeck Museum where the meeting will be held (the meeting is with the John Steinbeck Rotary Club) and nose around a bit, looking for ideas.

Back at the office, Mark leaves to go pick up a high school girl who needs a ride to the meeting (what did I tell you?) and we arrange to meet back at the museum at 6 p.m.

After a bit of socializing and some introductions, the meeting is called to order by the president of the club—Mark Kimber (something he neglected to mention). There is an invocation and everyone salutes the flag—as my own small protest I choose not to say "under God"—and the business part of the meeting goes forward. This includes formal introductions of visiting Rotarians and other guests, including two high school students. One, a girl from Norway, has been here in Salinas for a year, living with local families, and is about to go home. Another, the girl Mark had to go pick up, is a graduating senior who had been abroad during her junior year—in Norway, I think—and will graduate as the class salutatorian. Mark notes, after checking with the girl to be sure she won't be embarrassed by having it mentioned, that she is the first in her family to graduate from high school. Now, he adds, she has been accepted, with full scholarship, to UC Berkeley. The girls' presence, it's clear, means their year-abroad trips were fully paid for by this club.

Other announcements are made, including one about the club's purchase and distribution of a thousand dictionaries to local third-graders, a program begun after a study showed that introduction to a dictionary at a young age is one of the best ways to combat illiteracy.

Other announcements happen and some awards are presented, all of it salted with witty comments from President Mark, and the aura of goodwill and the genuine pleasure in good works that permeates the evening is very impressive.

I had decided to wait and learn what these folks are about and try to be appropriately responsive to what I see, so when Mark introduces me I get to thank them not only for their tradition of service, but for the generosity and thoughtfulness that have made it so meaningful—to these kids, for example—on a personal level.

Noting that the name John Steinbeck plays such an important part here, not only in the place they meet but in the name of their organization, I cite *The Grapes of Wrath* and Tom Joad's discovery that maybe "a fella ain't got a soul of his own, but on'y a piece of a big one—the one big soul that belongs to ever'body . . ." and that what this meant to him was the determination to "be ever'where—wherever you look. Wherever they's a fight so hungry people can eat, I'll be there. Wherever they's a cop beatin' up a guy, I'll be there. I'll be in the way guys yell when they're mad—an' I'll be in the way kids laugh when they're hungry an' they know supper's ready. An' when our people eat the stuff they raise an' live in the houses they build, why, I'll be there."

Then I remind them that at a darker time, here in this very town that they love, Steinbeck's books were burned. These great works of art, these celebrations of the human spirit, ignited so much revulsion in fearful people that they were destroyed. So it's part of our job to see the bigger picture as well as the little one, to take pride in the fact that kids get dictionaries, but to remember the kids who don't get them too, and the families whose kids still don't graduate from school.

One of my favorite Steinbeck passages comes from his book *Sweet Thursday,* where he says the big question is, "What has my life meant so far, and what can it mean in the time left to me? . . . What have I contributed in the Great Ledger?"

Holding up a folder, I smile. "Mark said I could speak to anything I wanted this evening. I have here a twenty-six-page speech on human rights and a twenty-three page speech on the death penalty. But I think it's more appropriate this evening to simply thank you for the service you're doing, these things that are clearly a meaningful contribution to the Great Ledger, and just underscore Mr. Steinbeck's observation about 'the one big soul that belongs to everybody.' With all the good we do, there remains more to be done. With all that's been done for these, it's important to remember the ones who are left behind and make sure they're not forgotten."

There was more, and then a Q&A. And we ended up having a lot of fun.

Mark was good to his word and the meeting ends at just about 8:30. After some pictures are taken and some parting words are exchanged, I fire up Mule and we head south. I call Shelley from the highway at around 9 and say I'm hoping to get home tonight, but it might be as late as 3 a.m., so not to be alarmed if I come crashing in at that hour.

She's worried about my being too tired, so I assure her if I start to lose it I'll pull into a motel and call her.

But Mule must have smelled the corral, because she takes off and flies low. We pull into the house at 1:30 in the morning and she isn't even breathing hard.

God, does it feel good to be home!

CONCLUSION

Thursday, June 12–Saturday, June 14, 2008

LOS ANGELES, CA

END OF TOUR

T hursday was a blur. Happy to be home, I was in a stupor for most of the day, vibrating as if I was still on the road, utterly useless. Shelley was beautiful as ever—maybe more so—and excited and thrilled that I was home in one piece. My sweet daughter Erin and our lovely friend Patricia, who had teamed up to take such good care of Shelley that she was up and around with only the assistance of a cane, now kept an eye on me to be sure I didn't walk into a wall. You know how you can get yourself psyched up for a tough job and only when it's over do you allow the stress of it all to crash in on you? Well, that was me. I did manage to go outside a couple of times to say hello to Mule and unload a few things, but that was pretty much it. I studiously avoided looking at the avalanche of mail awaiting my attention, spoke mostly in grunts, stared into space and tried to ignore the whirling in my brain.

In the evening, Shelley and I sat down to watch the Lakers run up a twenty-four-point lead over the Celtics in a dazzling demonstration of ability guaranteeing that they'd even up the series—only to sit there slack-jawed as they managed to LOSE again.

By Friday it was almost possible to think. Still vibrating, I was finally able to unload Mule and take her out to have a friend look at her crown to make sure she didn't have any lasting effects from the Louisiana railroad track incident. Not a scratch. Am I surprised to learn she has a hard head?

Checking with Hertz to see if I can return her to a more convenient location than going all the way back to LAX airport, I'm told I cannot without paying a bunch of extra money. Okay, LAX is a pain in the ass, but it isn't that bad. But I'm also told that if I don't get her there by 2 p.m.—not possible since it's already 1:40—I'll have to pay for an extra day. Fine. I'm not in a big hurry to say goodbye to her anyway.

Saturday morning, my lovely daughter Erin agrees to meet me at LAX and bring me home after returning Mule. As I get ready to leave, Shelley says she'd like to sit in her once before she's gone. As she settles in the passenger seat, I go through the now-familiar routine to start the engine so she can experience the silence of the electric motor. Shelley is charmed by Mule and wants a ride, so we go back and forth in the driveway for a bit, Mule beeping as we do. Then she wants to try it in the backseat. I'm happy that she's so appreciative, and Mule is virtually purring with delight as we go back and forth again, Shelley now Miss Daisy.

My sweet wife is knocked out, says so, and it's clearly a mutual admiration society.

But, time to go. Shelley waves goodbye and Mule honks as we head for the road once again.

The 405 is a mess as usual, and Mule is too busy to talk. It's just as well, I guess; no need to make her jittery. But I do want her to know how grateful I am for the way she has taken care of me. How do you say thank you to a critter who carried you 8,882 miles, through twenty-nine states, through deserts and mountains, heat and cold, sunshine and downpour, dancing around tornadoes and floods, all in just under five weeks' time? And did it without—well, almost without—complaint.

This has been a truly extraordinary—certainly life-enhancing if not life-changing—process; engaging with hundreds, maybe thousands of people in states called red and blue, offering thoughts and experiences, challenging viewpoints, and asking consideration of ideas that may be foreign to their lives. To do this and encounter such warmth and generosity, such an open and grateful embrace—even from those who may feel differently—is to have reaffirmed my belief that there is a core of decency and fairness alive in this land, a recognition that the values we all cherish do point in the same direction even if we sometimes become confused or misguided. There is a fundamental truth in the knowledge that all human beings do want the same things: love, attention and respect; and this understanding is what created the spirit of America.

"And you, Mule, have made this adventure possible. You've been my guide and protector, my Rocinante."

Snort.

"Yeah, I know. Sorry."

Silence.

"Well, old pal, here we are. Recognize this place?"

A quiver.

"Yup. They'll give you a wash and polish, curry and comb, lube and oil. Maybe some new shoes."

Another quiver.

As we pull up, Erin is waiting. She gets in and we move into the line that says *RETURN*. Men direct us into the proper spot and then it's all business as we get out; a guy checks the papers, jots down the mileage, hands the papers back, directs us to Customer Service and walks away.

A last look, a touch. "Love you, Mule."

Silence.

As we walk away toward Customer Service, I hear just a whisper, "Bye, Mike."

Resource Guide

ACLU of Colorado
400 Corona St.
Denver, CO 80218
tel: 303-777-5482; fax: 303-777-1773
info@aclu-co.org
www.aclu-co.org

ACLU of Maryland
3600 Clipper Mill Rd., Suite 350
Baltimore, MD 21211
tel: 410-889-8555
aclu@aclu-md.org
www.aclu-md.org

ACLU of Michigan
2966 Woodward Ave.
Detroit, MI 48201
tel: 313-578-6800; fax: 313-578-6811
aclu@aclumich.org
www.aclumich.org

ACLU of Pennsylvania
313 Atwood St.
Pittsburgh, PA 15213
tel: 412-681-7736
info@aclupgh.org
www.aclupa.org

American Friends Service Committee (Middle Atlantic Region)
4806 York Rd.
Baltimore, MD 21212
tel: 410-323-7200; fax: 410-323-7292
mar@afsc.org
www.afsc.org

Brooklyn for Peace
41 Schermerhorn St., PMB 106
Brooklyn, NY 11201
tel/fax: 718-624-5921
bpfp@brooklynpeace.org
www.brooklynpeace.org

Buncombe Green Party
tel: 828-225-4347
hoosier848@yahoo.com
www.buncombegreens.org

Center for Constitutional Rights
667 Broadway, 7th Fl.
New York, NY 10012
tel: 212-614-6443
info@ccrjustice.org
www.ccrjustice.org

Center for Victims of Torture (Minneapolis Healing Center)
717 E. River Pkwy.
Minneapolis, MN 55455
tel: 612-436-4800; fax 612-436-2600
cvt@cvt.org | www.cvt.org

Centerforce

2955 Kerner Blvd., 2nd Floor
San Rafael, CA 94901
tel: 415-456-9980
www.centerforce.org

Coalition of Arizonans to Abolish the Death Penalty

PO Box 77312
Tucson, AZ 85703
tel: 602-400-4025
info@azabolitionist.org
www.azabolitionist.org

Death Penalty Focus

870 Market St., Suite 859
San Francisco, CA 94102
tel: 415-243-0143; fax: 415-243-0994
info@deathpenalty.org
www.deathpenalty.org

El Pasoans Against the Death Penalty

tel: 915-532-0527
elpaso@tcadp.org

Greenpeace

702 H St., NW
Washington, DC 20001
tel: 202-462-1177
info@wdc.greenpeace.org
www.greenpeace.org

Human Rights Watch (San Francisco)
100 Bush St., Suite 1812
San Francisco, CA 94104
tel: 415-362-3250; fax: 415-362-3255
hrwsf@hrw.org
www.hrw.org

John Steinbeck Rotary Club
National Steinbeck Center
1 Main St.
Salinas, CA 93901
tel: 831-775-4721; fax: 831-796-3828
info@steinbeck.org
www.steinbeck.org

Military Religious Freedom Foundation
13170-B Central Ave., SE, Suite 255
Albuquerque, NM 87123
tel: 800-736-5109
info@militaryreligiousfreedom.org
www.militaryreligiousfreedom.org

Minnesota Democratic-Farmer-Labor Veterans' Caucus
tel: 616-822-9067
www.mndflvets.org

Nation Magazine
33 Irving Pl.
New York, NY 10003
tel: 212-209-5400; fax: 212-982-9000
info@thenation.com
www.thenation.com

North Carolina Justice Center
224 S. Dawson St.
Raleigh, NC 27601
tel: 919-856-2570; fax: 919-856-2175
contact@ncjustice.org
www.ncjustice.org

Peace, Education, and Action Center of Eastern Iowa (PEACE Iowa)
Old Brick
26 E. Market St.
Iowa City, IA 52245
tel: 319-354-1925
peaceiowa@iowatelecom.net
www.peaceiowa.org

People of Faith Against the Death Penalty
110 W. Main St., Suite 2G
Carrboro, NC 27510
tel: 919-933-7567; fax: 919-933-5611
info@pfadp.org
www.pfadp.org

Public Citizen
1600 20th St., NW
Washington, DC 20009
tel: 202-588-1000
member@citizen.org
www.citizen.org

Service Employees International Union (S.E.I.U.)
1800 Massachusetts Ave., NW
Washington, DC 20036

S.E.I.U. continued

tel: 202-730-7000
info@seiu.org
www.seiu.org

Society of the Muse of the Southwest (SOMOS)

229 Paseo del Pueblo Sur, PO Box 3225
Taos, NM 87571
tel: 575-758-0081; fax: 575-758-4802
somos@laplaza.org
www.somostaos.org

Southern Center for Human Rights

83 Poplar St., NW
Atlanta, GA 30303
tel: 404-688-1202; fax: 404-688-9440
rights@schr.org
www.schr.org

Texas Coalition to Abolish the Death Penalty

2709 S. Lamar Blvd.
Austin, TX 78704
tel: 512-441-1808
info@tcadp.org
www.tcadp.org

UNM—Taos Library

115 Civic Plaza Dr.
Taos, NM 87571
tel: 575-737-6242; fax: 575-737-6292
unmtlib@unm.edu
taos.unm.edu/library

Veterans for Peace, Phoenix
15825 S. 28th Pl.
Phoenix, AZ 85048
tel: 602-400-9179
ekjh7470@cox.net
www.veteransforpeacephoenix.org

Veterans for Peace (Chapter 099)
PO Box 456
Mars Hill, NC 28754
tel: 828-400-1145
ken@veterans4peace.org
www.veterans4peace.org